Cockpit Follies

by Garth Wallace

Published by
Happy Landings

Keep smiling!
Garth

Other books by Garth Wallace:

Fly Yellow Side Up
Pie In The Sky
Derry Air
Blue Collar Pilots
Don't Call Me a Legend
The Flying Circus

Canadian Catalogue Data:

Cockpit Follies
fiction, aviation, humour

Written by:
Wallace, Garth 1946 -

ISBN 0-969-7322-8-7

C813'.54

Editing:
Liz Wallace

Cover and inside artwork:
Francois Bougie

Layout and typesetting
Amadeo Gaspar

Written, typeset, printed and bound
in Canada

Published by:

Happy Landings
RR #4
Merrickville, Ontario
K0G 1N0
Tel.: 613-269-2552
Fax: 613-269-3962
E-mail: books@happylanding.com
Web site: www.happylanding.com

Cockpit Follies

Contents

Introduction

This is your captain speaking; fasten your seat belts and get ready to laugh. *Cockpit Follies* is a humorous, inside look at the world of aviation from the best seat in the house: the pilot's seat. On this flight you will meet Blowhard Bull Muldoone, Edgar the Astronaut, Inspector Crusty, Marathon Melville, Elmer the Snitch and more. The names of these characters have been changed but they know who they are and by the end of this book so will you.

When reading about road circuits and hydro pole slaloms you might think that these pilots don't fly for any airline that you have been on. Don't be so sure. The next time you board a flight, have a peak in the cockpit. If a *Cockpit Follies* character is sitting in the pilot's seat, say "Hello" from me.

Garth Wallace

Dedication

Cockpit Follies is dedicated to all student pilots.
Thank you for the memories.

Chapter One

Pink fuel

On the day of her first lesson, I was waiting for a "Mrs. Muldoone" by the front desk of the flying school office. Soon a tall, shapely woman on the other side of middle age strutted through the door. Her hair was bottle blonde and her high-mileage face was covered in industrial strength make-up. A pink sweater and skirt were purposefully too small and the spikes on her hooker heels would have dimpled the strongest aircraft wing-walk. I assessed her as an air-headed trophy bride.

She zeroed in on me right away. "Good morning," she said cheerfully, "are you my instructor?"

"Mrs. Muldoone? Yes, I am."

"Gin," she said immediately, holding out her hand. A collection of bracelets rattled on her arm. "Call me Gin."

"Okay Gin, pleased to meet you."

"I'm really looking forward to this," she said immediately. "I've always wondered why Bull liked flying around in little airplanes." She waved her bracelets toward the Cherokees parked on the flightline and wrinkled her nose when she said, "little airplanes." I decided I was about to waste her time and her husband's money.

Bull Muldoone had booked his wife on the school's "Pitch Hitter Flying Course." Muldoone was the blowhard owner of a Piper Twin Comanche parked in our hangar. The Pitch Hitter Course was designed for pilot spouses. Instruction on straight and level flying, map reading and radio work were given so a pilot's companion could participate in a flight. The course also taught how to radio for help and to land the airplane in case the pilot became incapacitated in the air.

I wasn't sure why Muldoone wanted his wife on the course. The overweight, cigar-chewing loudmouth was a good candidate for a heart attack but I had never seen his wife fly with him.

7

Derry Air's no-nonsense receptionist, Angel, had told me that I was booked with "Mrs. Muldoone."

"On their Twin Comanche?" I had asked excitedly. Multi-engine flying time was like gold for flying instructors with their sights on the airlines.

"No, on a Cherokee."

"Oh."

I didn't like the thought of flying with such an unmotivated student but at this school, if you were booked for a lesson, you flew.

"How do we get started?" Gin asked. She made it sound like she was interested.

"First, we'll sit down over here and I'll outline the course," I said, motioning toward a briefing cubicle.

I sat Gin across from me at a table and showed her the lesson plan for the Pitch Hitter Course. She propped her elbows, meshed her fingers together and rested her chin on them. She watched me with a steady stare. I spoke slowly hoping she could follow what I was saying.

"I'll show you how to read an aviation map and how to talk on the radio," I said. I was thinking that she probably wished she was shopping and not at the airport.

"Do I get to fly the plane?" she asked.

"Yes. In fact today I'll have you steering the airplane in straight and level flight but don't worry, there are dual controls so I can fly along with you."

"Good, but I'm not worried," she replied quickly. "If you knew me, you'd worry for you, not me."

I wasn't sure what she was talking about but I smiled in case it was a joke. I finished outlining the course without asking questions. I didn't want to overtax her minimal interest in aviation. We headed outside.

"I'll show you some of the things a pilot checks on the airplane before flying," I offered.

"Okay."

I started at the door on the right side of the Cherokee. "The airplane is made of aluminum," I explained, "which is lighter and more corrosion resistant than steel."

"Like my Cobra," Gin commented.

"A Mustang Cobra?"

"No, a Shelby AC Cobra," she replied. "The aluminum is light but the body gets dinged bad if I take it to the mall."

If she had it right, Gin was driving what had been the fastest production car in the world and one of the most expensive.

I continued the walkaround inspection and showed her the basic aircraft controls. At the front of the wing, I removed the fuel cap. "Look in and you'll see the fuel level. The tab indicates about two-thirds full."

"The gas is pink!" she exclaimed.

It was an appropriate bimbo comment. I wanted to say that we provided our customers with their choice of designer fuel colours. Instead, I said, "That tells the pilot that the fuel is 80 octane."

"I buy 100 octane in barrels from the local fuel dealer for the Cobra," she said. "It's green. I have to hand pump it but if I don't use it, the car runs like crap on the stuff from the gas station."

I was starting to change my first impression of Gin. I replaced the fuel cap and pointed to the engine cowling. "If you open that flap on top of the engine and unscrew the dipstick, we can check the oil."

She readily popped the flap and looked inside. "There's not much in here," she commented.

"It's a four-cylinder, 150-horsepower engine," I offered.

"What's the displacement?"

"Three hundred and twenty cubic inches."

"The Cobra has a 427 V-8 putting out three times the horsepower. Are you sure this thing'll fly?"

"It's a training airplane," I replied. "Bull's Twin Comanche has two of those engines."

"How fast will the Comanche go?"

"Maximum speed is 180 miles per hour."

"Same as the Cobra."

Gin checked the oil. "It's at five," she said. She was sharp enough not to pull the stick right out and drip oil on her pink outfit.

"That's good," I said. "We add one at four."

"Four what?"

"Quarts," I replied. "American quarts."

We continued around the airplane.

"Those dinky tires look awful bald," she observed.

"Stingy Mingy won't let the mechanics replace them until the chord is showing." The reference to my tight-fisted boss slipped out by accident.

"Stingy Mingy, I like it," Gin said with a grin. "What is your name for Bull?"

I could feel my face turning red.

"Come on," she said. "I won't tell him."

"The Pineapple," I replied.

"Perfect!" she exclaimed. "Prickly on the outside and a hole for a brain: I've got my own names for him, but I like 'Pineapple'."

"We don't need much trend on the tires," I offered, trying to bring the lesson back on track. "We don't use them for traction or high speed turns."

"Well, not much tread is what you got. They don't even look like they're radials."

"They're not."

We finished the pre-flight inspection at the entrance door. "Climb on board and slide over to the pilot's seat on the left side," I said.

The tight pink skirt made it a difficult manoeuvre but Gin wasn't shy. I saw acres of leg but she got the job done. While I was climbing in beside her, she looked around the cabin. "It'd be tough getting lucky in one of these things." She made it sound like an observation and not an invitation.

"Yeah, but it's great for teaching flying."

"I'm just trying to figure out why Bull likes to spend every day at the airport."

I didn't comment. I spent every day at the airport. I rarely saw Bull.

I started the Cherokee, called ground control and taxied out for take-off, explaining briefly what I was doing along the way. Gin continued to ask intelligent questions. We took off, climbed out and cleared the airport control zone. I had her take control. She quickly mastered the technique of guiding the airplane with a light touch rather than overcontrolling it. There was time left over at the end of the lesson.

"Do you want to see your house from the air on the way back to the airport?" I asked.

"Sure, it's on the ridge east of town. Look for the biggest, god-awful monument to classless wealth that you've ever seen."

"Is it a white Spanish-style villa?"

"You've seen it."

"I watched it being built from the air. There was a line-up of cement trucks along the road for weeks."

Gin nodded knowingly. "I call it, 'the bunker'."

The sun was out and I could see the white square of concrete in the distance. As we drew closer, I could make out the bright red roof, the cement and wrought iron perimeter fence and the two giant white cement bulls guarding the entrance.

"How low can we fly?" Gin asked, looking down at the house. Her voice had taken on a hard edge.

"One thousand feet over a built-up area," I replied. We were flying about two thousand feet above the ground. "Do you want to fly lower?"

"Yes," she said, still staring at the house. "That pink Cadillac in the driveway belongs to Martha 'the mouth' Madden. She and Bull are in the sack. Now I know why he wanted me to take flying lessons."

I didn't know what to say. Gin didn't sound angry but the discovery couldn't have made her happy. I didn't say anything.

"I want to buzz the place so they know that I know they're there." Her cheerful tone was returning. She was forming a plan.

I didn't want to be in an airplane flown for the first time by a vengeful wife buzzing her two-timing husband. I didn't reply. She turned and

looked at me. She saw my fear. She smiled and said, "Come on, it'll be fun. He does this to me all the time. It's a chance to get him back. One quick low pass."

The estate was well separated from its neighbours. I had dual controls. "Okay, one quick low and over but nothing suicidal," I said.

"Don't worry about that," she said. Then she placed both hands on her control wheel and rolled the airplane on its left ear. The nose dropped until it was pointed straight at the two bulls by the driveway entrance. It was a smooth, coordinated manoeuvre.

I reached for the throttle and pulled it to idle. "We have redlines for the engine and airframe," I explained. "Don't dive any steeper. I'll add power when you level off."

"Okay," she said. The adrenaline was building in her voice. I hoped I wasn't making a big mistake.

Gin held the nose down. We dove below 1,000 feet accelerating through 130 miles per hour. The twin bulls got bigger in our windshield.

"Yahoo!" she yelped. There was a big grin on her face.

I held one hand on the throttle and the other ready on my control wheel. "Start levelling off," I barked over the increasing wind noise.

Gin let the nose rise. We zoomed over the cement gate guards at 140 mph. She levelled the airplane off 100 feet above the driveway. We were pointed straight at the red roof. I added full power.

"Fly over the house, not through," I said loudly.

Gin lifted the airplane's nose slightly.

"Bull, you turkey!" she yelled. "Hear this!"

The villa flashed by underneath. Gin hauled back on the control wheel and pointed the Cherokee skyward.

"I hope he was in full flight," she said excitedly.

I pointed at the rapidly decaying airspeed on the indicator. "Level off and head toward the airport," I said.

Gin pushed forward on the control wheel and banked left. "I'll get a lot of mileage out of that one," she said. "Thanks a lot."

"You're welcome."

I didn't touch the controls for the rest of the flight. I talked Gin into the airport traffic pattern and through the approach and landing.

"That was great!" she exclaimed when the engine was shut down. "When can we go again?"

"I'm glad you liked it," I replied. "We'll check the booking sheets inside."

While Angel was making out Gin's bill, I set up another lesson with her in two days.

"Thanks again," she said. "I really enjoyed that."

"So did I," I replied sincerely. "See you Thursday."

The next morning Angel said that the flying school owner Irving Mingy wanted to see me in his office, "Right away."

I walked through the open door behind the reception area. The straight-faced owner was sitting in the only chair hunched over a ledger on his desk.

"You wanted to see me?"

"I got a call from an irate Bull Muldoone," he said quietly. He didn't look up. "He thought he was sending his wife on a flying lesson yesterday, not a reconnaissance mission."

I didn't know what to say. I stood nervously waiting to be fired.

Mingy looked up from his desk. "He suggested for her lesson tomorrow that you take her up to 5,280 feet and keep her more suitably occupied."

Now I was really speechless.

"As long as she is messing around, he can do the same," he added.

I swallowed hard. I could feel the sweat forming on my brow.

"You can relax," Mingy continued. Then his face broke into a rare smile. "At Derry Air we aim to please but there's a limit. I just wanted you to know that I booked Mrs. Muldoone with another pilot."

I let out a long breath. "Well thank you, sir, I think. Who's going to fly with her?"

His grin widened. "Me."

Chapter Two

Spin wimp

"How about a checkout on the Warrior?" Eric Daedalus asked me. Eric was the chief flying instructor. He was referring to the latest addition to the flying school fleet. We flew Piper Cherokee 140s for training but Derry Air owner Irving Mingy had purchased a Piper Warrior. Eric knew I was sitting out a student cancellation.

"I've flown Warriors before," I said politely. I thought I'd save Eric the trouble and the company the expense of checking me out.

"I know, but I haven't," Eric replied. "This will be my checkout."

Eric was a friendly, easy-to-work-for boss. I was happy to oblige. "Okay, let's go," I said.

"I'll be ready in a minute," he replied. Then he disappeared into his office. A minute later he came out carrying two packed parachutes. "Here." He held one out for me.

"No thanks," I said, smiling nervously. I was hoping he was kidding. "I heard your flying was bad but it can't be that bad."

"Wise guy. I'm serious. I want to check out all the Warrior's flying characteristics," he said.

"We can do that without parachutes," I replied.

"Including spins," he added.

"Eric, spinning is prohibited in a Warrior."

"Right. It's not certified for intentional spins. That's why we're going to spin it. I want to find out why it's not certified."

I shook my head back and forth. "Piper has test pilots. Call them. In the meantime I'd be happy to fly a regular checkout with you."

"I read about the flight testing on the Warrior. It spins and recovers just fine but Piper ducked the cost of certifying it for spins."

"There you go. Believe what you read and we'll skip the spins."

I wasn't afraid of the spins. I was afraid of Eric. He was an ex-paratrooper whose idea of fun was to play "UFO" by skydiving at night over the city holding flares. I had never jumped out of an airplane in the air and didn't want to start but our conversation was attracting the attention of other staff. The two instructors giving ground briefings to students in the cubicles along the wall were looking our way. Two other instructors on a coffee break by the front window had stopped their conversation.

Eric continued to hold out the parachute. "I want to tell the staff how it spins and recovers."

I ignored the offering. "Fine. You can do that after I check you out."

"I want to see how it spins with a student and instructor. You're the only body available."

"If I'm going to need a parachute, I don't want to go," I said firmly.

"You won't need it. It's a formality," Eric said, smiling. "We're not going to do anything that a student pilot wouldn't do."

"One of your students or mine?" I was stalling.

"Come on. If you don't like what we're doing, we'll come back to the airport right away."

I had worked at Derry Air long enough to know that Eric was a joker. He would say that just to make me go. I knew the conversation was wrecking my macho flying instructor image but I didn't budge.

"There is nothing you can say that will make me climb into a perfect-ly good airplane wearing a parachute," I declared.

"I'll count it as revenue flying hours on your pay," he offered.

Eric knew which button to push. I hesitated.

"At double the rate," he added.

The other staff members were watching. I took the parachute.

"There. That didn't hurt, did it?" Eric said in a patronizing voice.

"Not yet," I replied.

Eric signed the flight sheets, picked up the Warrior's logbook and took the keys from the receptionist. "Angel, mark this as revenue hours for my dummy student here".

"Double time," I added.

The burly spinster looked at the parachutes. "I won't mark it revenue until you come back," she replied.

We walked out to the airplane. "I get the right seat," I said.

"No, you're the student on this exercise. The student rides left."

"The door is on the right," I replied. "Just pretend that I'm a student instructor."

"Nothing is going to happen," Eric said smoothly. "You won't need to jump out."

I had him this time. "Good. Then you won't mind flying in the left seat."

"Okay," Eric conceded, "but if we need to hit the silk, I'll give you

15

three milliseconds to clear that door or they'll find you in the wreck with my footprints on your head."

We divided up the walkaround inspection. I took the left side. When I looked into the fuel tank, I could see it was full. "Shouldn't the fuel be down to the tabs to be in the utility category?" I asked.

"Yah, but I told Huey to fill it up," he said. "If we flat spin on partial tanks, the centrifugal force uncovers the fuel inlets and the engine quits."

"I thought you said it spun conventionally."

"It will. It will," he said quickly. "That's why I picked you to go along. We'll be nose heavy. It shouldn't flat spin." He was not convincing me. "It won't flat spin," he added. "I'm sure it won't."

"Now we have two rules," I declared. "No flat spins and we come back when I say."

"Scout's honour," he replied.

We finished the inspection.

The parachutes were fanny packs. Before he got in, Eric helped me put on my pack and adjust the straps. Once everything was attached, I was locked into a sitting position while still standing up. Eric showed me the rip chord. "If we have to jump, I'll yell, 'Go, go, go!' On the third 'go', you should be gone. Don't pull this until you're falling clear of the airplane or you're close to the ground, whichever comes first."

Eric climbed into the Warrior. His chute was made for him and the pilot seat on the Warrior was adjustable down to make more headroom. Eric was shorter than I. He had no trouble fitting into the airplane with the chute on. I followed by crawling on the wing and falling, backside first, into the right seat. The height of the seat was not adjustable. My head was pressed against the ceiling. The sun visor filled most of my forward view.

Eric started the engine and asked for taxi instructions for a local flight. I fought with the seatbelt. The only way I could do it up was to fully extend the lap adjustment and yank hard.

"You look like one of those college students trying to set a record for the most people in a Volkswagen," Eric said with a grin.

"I feel like one of them."

I sat crammed into the seat thinking that it would be impossible for me to jump out of this airplane. I couldn't move enough to force the door open against the slipstream and propel myself out. I sat wedged with my head cocked to one side so I could see what was going on.

Eric flew a couple of circuits trying short and soft field takeoffs and landings. He was a smooth pilot. He made a few notes on his kneepad. We departed the circuit and climbed out to 4,000 feet.

"Ready for a stall?" he asked.

"Sure. I'm not going anywhere."

Eric completed some safety checks. He reduced the power and pulled the nose up. The stall horn sounded, the airframe buffeted and the nose dropped. Eric relaxed his back pressure and added power. The Warrior flew out of the stall immediately. We lost less than 200 feet.

"Piece of cake," Eric said.

"Fine," I said. "Let's go back."

"Not yet."

He flew a couple of more stalls in different configurations of flap and power. The airplane's reaction was gentle and conventional each time. We lost very little altitude. It seemed like a nice flying, forgiving airplane.

Eric climbed the willing Warrior to 5,000 feet. "Ready for a spin?"

I put my hand on the door handle. "Ready when you are."

He cut the power, raised the nose and applied left rudder. The Warrior skidded into a spiral. Eric recovered. "I'll try it again with more rudder," he said.

"Okay."

This time he booted full left rudder. The airplane hesitated and then slid into a spiral.

"I'll try one to the right," Eric said during the recovery.

During the next spin attempt he shoved the right rudder before the stall. The airplane dropped its right wing as if to spin but then the descent flattened into a spiral.

"I guess that's why Piper didn't certify it for spins," Eric said. "It won't spin. Ready to head back?"

"Let me try one," I offered.

Eric didn't know it, but I had taught aerobatics at a previous flying school.

"It's okay," he replied. "If it doesn't want to go, no sense forcing it."

It was the first time I had heard a lack of bravado coming from the former paratrooper. He sounded like he was wimping out.

"I'll try one," I said. "If it doesn't work, we'll go back."

I took control before Eric let go. He opened his mouth to speak. I rammed in full power, hauled back on the control wheel and pitched the Warrior into a steep climbing turn to the right.

"Wait..." he started to say.

I had never heard the squeaky little voice coming from Eric. I shoved in full left rudder. The airplane rewarded my rough handling by snapping into a vicious spin to the left. The rotation was so violent that it initially carried the Warrior onto its back. Dirt, gravel and lost pencils floated into view during the momentary negative gravity. I remained firmly wedged in my seat but Eric's belts were not as tight. A big "Whoaa..." of surprise was cut short when his head slammed into the ceiling.

I cut the power and held the Warrior in the spin.

"Eeeeeee!" Eric was trying to stifle a scream.

The Warrior rotated closer to right side up after spinning a turn and a half. I fed in opposite rudder and neutralized the stabilator. The spin stopped at two turns and entered a dive. I pulled back. Eric smacked down into his seat.

I turned to look at him. "That's why Piper didn't certify it for spins," I declared. Eric looked stunned. I was having fun. "Let's try one to the right," I said enthusiastically.

"No!" Eric yelped.

I ignored him and yanked the Warrior into a steep climbing turn to the left and added full power.

"I have control!" he bellowed.

Too late. I was already booting the right rudder. Over we went.

The paratrooper didn't like it. He emitted little squeaks of fear while pressing his right hand against the Warrior's roof to prevent falling on his head. I looked over at him on the recovery. His eyes were wide. I had

never seen him like this.

I levelled off. "I didn't mean to scare you, Eric. Wait 'til the guys on the ground hear about this."

Eric gathered himself up and grabbed the wheel with his left hand. "I have control," he said firmly.

I let go of my controls. Eric placed the Warrior in a full sideslip with left wing down and right rudder. He raised the nose with his left hand and then reached over and undid my seatbelt. Before I could say anything, he put his hand over my head and popped the door latch. The wind noise filled the cabin. The low pressure of the sideslip forced the top of the door open. Eric grabbed my shoulder as if to shove me out. "I don't think the guys on the ground are going to hear about it!" he yelled. "Do you?"

"No!"

Chapter Three

Bent out of shape

Mark Warren discovered that the vertical fin of a Piper Cherokee 140 didn't fit under the wing of a McDonnell Douglas DC-9. Warren was a Derry Air rental customer with a high-strung personality. He was a radio advertising salesman in a perpetual hurry. One of the first things he did after receiving his pilot licence was rent a Derry Air Cherokee and fly to Toronto International, the busiest airport in Canada.

Derry Air did not allow newly-licenced private pilots to take its aircraft to Toronto International. Warren avoided the rule by telling Angel that he was going to Brampton. It was an acceptable destination in the same direction.

The purpose of Warren's trip was to drop off his brother who was catching an overseas airline flight from Toronto. Warren got there all right. His passenger hopped out at the general aviation door under one of the airline terminal gates. Warren swung the Cherokee around to depart. He tried to taxi under the wing of a parked DC-9. The trailing edge of the 9's left aileron neatly sliced the plastic cap off the 140's vertical fin and rudder.

The manoeuvre must have been accompanied by the sound of ripping fibreglass and tearing metal as well as a lurch when the top of the Cherokee's tail snagged the airliner. This didn't stop the man-in-a-hurry. He simply applied more power and continued on his way. Apparently no one on the ground saw it happen. It is a tribute to the Piper design that the airplane did not shed the rest of its tail on the flight back.

Warren flew to Derry, parked the Cherokee on the flying school ramp and returned the logbook and keys to Angel. He charged the flight to a credit card and breezed out the door without saying anything about the damage.

Flying instructor Henry Rains was booked on the same aircraft with a student that afternoon. During the walkaround, Henry couldn't believe his eyes. The top of the fin and rudder looked like they had been hacked off with a dull axe. Wire for the missing rotating beacon and rear navigation light hung over the jagged edge.

While Henry stood there with his mouth open, his student completed the walkaround and said, "All set?"

Henry looked at him for a full thirty seconds before answering. "Didn't you find anything wrong with the airplane?" Henry asked slowly.

"No, it looks fine. Are we ready to go?"

"No."

Several things happened over the next hour. Henry reported the damage to Darcy Philips, Derry Air's chief mechanic. Angel juggled the bookings so Henry could have another aircraft. Most of the lesson was spent on an intense walkaround lecture.

Warren was called and asked about the wrecked tail. He denied any knowledge. Having flown with the perpetually distracted salesman during his lessons, I believed him.

Major Airlines, the owner of the DC-9, called. A ramp crewman had found pieces of a Cherokee under the airliner and reported them. Investigation revealed white Piper paint on the 9's aileron but no further damage. Records from the Toronto Control Tower led to Derry Air as the owner of the other aircraft. The head ramp agent called the flying school. He was looking for blood but was no match for Angel.

"One of your no-good, stupid, suicidal pilots unsuccessfully stuffed your aircraft under our DC-9."

"So," Angel replied.

"So? What do you mean, so? Don't you realize that the resulting damage could have jeopardized the lives of hundreds of passengers and crew, not to mention people on the ground, property damage, loss of equipment and harm to the airline's reputation?" The agent's anger was building. "What do you have to say about that?"

"Yes."

"Yes? That's all you can say?" He was yelling now. "Look, we're going to sue you, put you out of business, have you thrown in jail and make sure you never operate an airplane again!" He took a breath. Angel stepped in.

"You're assuming," Angel answered calmly, "that we still own that airplane as indicated by the government's less-than-up-to-date database; that the DC-9 was not moving at the time, nor was it crowding the general aviation gate; that your ramp crew did not in any way cause the accident or that issuing threats on the telephone is not against federal law."

There was a long silence.

"Thank you for calling," Angel said and hung up.

Henry led the discussion at the flying instructor coffee break that afternoon. "I couldn't believe my student walked around that airplane without seeing the wrecked tail," he said shaking his head.

"It doesn't surprise me," Eric replied. "I'll bet a round of beer that most students would have missed it. That's why we monitor their pre-flight inspections."

"Come on, Eric," Larry, one of the other instructors, said. "There was a jagged hole at the top of the fin with wires hanging out."

"I know," the chief instructor replied, "but students get conditioned. We tell them what to look for but everything they see is okay."

"I'll take your bet," I offered. The conversation stopped and everyone stared at me. "Leave the Cherokee on the ramp and I'll send my next student out to inspect it. I'll bet the beer that he'll snag the wrecked tail."

"Who's the student?" Henry asked.

"Melville."

"I don't think Eric meant to include Melville when he said 'student'," Henry suggested.

"Sure," Eric replied, "the bet stands. If Melville rejects the airplane for any reason, I'll buy the beer."

With 100 hours of flying lessons, Melville Passmore was the highest time student at Derry Air. He was book dumb but farm smart. He couldn't read a tractor manual but he could field strip and reassemble a Ford 8N in the dark. Melville was struggling badly with the academics of learning to fly but was quick to grasp the practical. He was so good with mechanical things that Dutch, Derry Air's ground school instructor, had the grubby little farm boy teaching engines and airframes in his class. If there was any student who could win Eric's bet for me, it was Melville.

When he arrived for his lesson, we did a ground briefing. Eric listened from the next cubicle to make sure I wasn't giving away the gig. When we were done, I signed us out to go flying.

"We're in Tango Victor Hotel today, Melville," I said, accepting the logbook and keys from Angel. "Let's go check it over."

"Okay," he replied enthusiastically. Melville was always excited about flying.

We walked out to the short-tailed Cherokee together. I could see a couple of instructors watching us from inside the lounge. Melville climbed into the aircraft, checked the fuel gauges, dropped the flaps, grabbed the fuel bottle and climbed out. He inspected the right wing, drained some fuel, opened the engine cowling, checked the oil and looked at the nose. Melville always appeared to take the pre-flight seriously. He inspected the airplane top to bottom, bustling around and under it with his long tongue trailing out the side of his mouth. He continued along the left wing, checking everything thoroughly. He walked beside the rear fuselage, checked the static port for the instruments and then looked at the tail. He

hesitated when he spotted the shorn vertical fin. Then he looked at me. I pretended to be interested in something else. He stood there contemplating the tail for a moment with his thumbs hooked in his coverall straps and his tongue hanging out. Then he continued inspecting the rest of the airplane. When he had worked his way up to the entrance door on the right side, he looked at the tail again and then hauled in his tongue and asked, "Are we ready to go?"

I couldn't believe it. Derry Air's most experienced student wanted to climb into that broken airplane and fly.

I had lost the bet but I wanted to test him further. "Are you ready to go?"

"Ready when you are," he replied promptly.

"What about the top of the rudder?" I asked.

Melville looked at it and said, "It's gone."

"No kidding. Didn't I teach you to check for damage on a walkaround?" I asked him loudly.

Melville stuffed his hands in his pockets and hung his head. He looked at the ground but didn't say anything.

"Didn't I?" I demanded.

"Yes," he said weakly. He didn't look up.

I was about to continue my inquisition when Eric came out of the office.

"I can guess what's going on out here," he said crossing the short distance to the airplane. The shy farm boy watched Eric approaching without lifting his head. "I'd like to make a point with you," he said to me, "if Melville doesn't mind."

Melville didn't say anything.

"Tell me, Melville, did you notice the damage on the tail during the walkaround?"

Melville replied quietly. "Yes."

"Why didn't you mention it?"

"I don't know." He sounded like a little kid caught with his hand in the cookie jar.

"Have you mentioned snags on walkarounds before?"

On this question, Melville lifted his head slightly. He looked at me and then at Eric.

"Yes."

"What happened?"

He didn't want to answer. He watched his feet and said nothing.

I wasn't sure where Eric was going with this but my anger was being replaced with curiousity.

"This is not a test, Melville. Nobody is going to yell at you," Eric said.

"When I asked about the bald tires," Melville replied slowly, "I was told, 'They'll last 'til the next inspection.' When I mentioned cracks in the windshield, I was told, 'They're okay.' Low fire extinguisher, 'Will still work.' When the oil is down, 'It's good enough for circuits.'"

I could hear myself saying these things to Melville. Eric's point was sinking in. I had conditioned Melville to ignore discrepancies.

"Would you fly this airplane solo today?" Eric asked.

"No," Melville said quickly.

"Would you fly it with an instructor?"

Melville shuffled his feet a little. "If he said it was okay."

"Well, it's not okay, Melville," Eric said gently. "Alpha November Delta is available. You guys can use it for your flight today." He turned to walk away.

"The wing is bent," Melville said quietly.

Eric stopped in his tracks. "What did you say?"

Melville stared at the ground and mumbled, "The left wing on Alpha November Delta is bent up more than the right."

The other Cherokee 140 was parked beside us on the ramp. Eric walked over and looked at it from the front. Melville and I followed. The airplane was definitely sitting a little crooked.

"I think the one oleo is lower than the other, Melville," Eric said.

The little round farmer walked toward the airplane, squatted on his haunches and pointed at the wing root underneath. "You can see where the skin has been pulled," he said.

Eric and I bent down beside him and looked. "I don't see anything," Eric said.

"You hafta look close."

Eric crawled under the wing and looked up. There were stretch lines in the wing panel under the main spar. There were little smiles of metal skin buckled against some of the rivet heads. The airplane must have been landed hard on that side.

"How long has it been like that?" Eric asked.

"Couple of months," Melville said quietly.

"That's why it spins differently left and right," I offered.

"I'll get Darcy out here," Eric said. "You guys find something else to do. We're out of airplanes." He headed off toward the hangar to find the chief mechanic.

"Let's wait to hear what Darcy says," I said to Melville. "Have you found anything wrong with the other aircraft?"

"Yes," he replied, looking at me shyly.

"Like what?"

"The scissors on the right gear leg of Tango Echo are cracked." He looked at me to see if he should keep going.

"And?"

"The tail skid on India Uniform has been punched into the fuselage."
I nodded for more.

"The chains on Tango Echo's control wheels are worn."

"How do you know that?"

"When I turn the control wheels in opposite directions, they move ten degrees."

"Well, there is only one other Cherokee in the fleet."

"Alpha Delta. Its propeller is out of track."

"How did you find that out?"

"I could feel it vibrate the last time I flew it so I checked the track against the engine nosebowl after the flight. It's out half an inch."

Darcy Philips and Eric appeared from the hangar. Darcy, always the jokester, called to Melville as he approached. "Is that the guy who's been wrecking our airplanes?"

Melville blushed.

"You'll see what I mean when you look under there," Eric said to Darcy.

The mechanic crawled under the left wing of November Delta. "Yup, she's been pulled all right." He jumped to his feet. "Thanks, Melville. You're pretty sharp to spot that." The young farmer beamed at the compliment. "With these two damaged Cherokees, my shop is going to be busy for weeks." He turned to Eric. "Both these airplanes are grounded. You guys are going to have to make do with the rest of the fleet."

"You don't know the half of it," I said.

Chapter Four

Moo

My wife Susan suggested that we host a Derry Air staff barbecue at our farm. I mentioned it to the fun-loving Eric Daedalus.

"A party? Great!" he said immediately. "We'll make it a Saturday evening. That won't interfere with the linecrews' regular Friday drink-up." He flipped open his datebook. "I guess this Saturday is too soon. How about in a couple of weeks?"

"Okay," I said. "Will you clear it with Mingy?"

He shot me a mocking look. "You forget that Irv owns this place but Angel runs it."

Eric talked to Angel, our iron maiden receptionist. He convinced her that a staff barbecue would be like a church social. She took over from there. She drew up a list of items, collared each staff member and assigned them a job. I drew a map to our farmhouse for Angel to photocopy and hand out. With spouses and children, the list topped 60 people.

I took the appointed day off and cut the grass. About mid-afternoon, several pick-up trucks arrived led by Darcy Philips and his mechanics from the Derry Air maintenance shop. They had driven around Derry and loaded up with picnic tables, lawn chairs and swing sets from various staff members.

They set up everything in our yard including a grill made from a 50-gallon steel drum cut open lengthwise. Angle-iron legs had been welded to it. I watched as a couple of mechanics filled this with charcoal which was then soaked from a jerry can of jet fuel. I backed away as one of the mechanics flicked a lighted match into the air over the barbecue. A mighty "swoosh" signalled the start of the party. The other half of the barrel had been made into a tub. This was filled with ice, beer and pop.

Susan and I did little as the hosts except greet people as they arrived. The kids played on the swings. Susan gave them each a ride around the

corral on "Glider," her quiet pony. A game of scrub baseball was orga-
nized in the pasture with occasional interference from our curious horses.
Burgers and hotdogs were cooked. Our German Shepherd, "Lady," made
friends with every little kid who was a potential food donor. Desserts
appeared on the serving table. Coffee was made in a big urn borrowed
from Angel's church. We all sat in a large circle around the backyard
while Eric presented Mingy with a wrapped gift. The kids had been told
that it was a mechanical snake set to spring out of a can disguised as
peanut brittle. Mingy played it well. He unwrapped the present and then
asked the kids, pointing the can at each one, if they would help him open
it. They shook their heads vigorously side to side. Some hid behind their
moms. When he finally unscrewed the lid, the cloth-covered steel spring
leaped out to a chorus of squeals.

The setting sun was a signal that the party was over. Everything was
packed up and carted away. By dark, Susan and I were left well thanked.
Our yard was clean, our German Shepherd was happily overstuffed and
our horses were lined up at the fence wondering where their new friends
had gone.

But hosting the party created a problem. The location of our farm was
burned on the mental map of every Derry Air flying instructor.

I was outside fixing the wooden fence in our backyard on my next day
off. Susan was at work. I heard an aircraft approaching and looked up. It

was a Piper Cherokee heading my way from the west. It was descending. The engine noise was increasing. I recognized it as one of the Derry Air airplanes. The descent continued well below any normal training altitude. The pilot was allowing the aircraft to gain speed. It was soon obvious that I was in for a royal buzz job.

The Cherokee levelled off about three metres above the ground. The pilot followed the dip in the pasture which put him below my altitude. He was headed straight for me. I climbed down from the fence. As the airplane approached, I could see a wide-eyed student in the left seat and a grinning Eric Daedalus in the right. They pulled up in time to clear the fence and the house behind me. They were close enough that I could see the little triangles of oil residue built up behind each rivet head on the Cherokee's belly as they passed overhead. The wings were rocking back and forth in a salute as the airplane climbed out toward the airport.

It was the first of five beat-ups that day. I know that at least two of them were by Eric. The first one was funny. The second one was amusing. After that, the horses, Lady and I thought they were a nuisance.

So did our neighbours. I was in the hardware store in the village that afternoon. Cecil Seymour, the local septic pump-out man was leaning against the counter in his brown-stained rubber boots, green work clothes and "Seymour Septic" cap.

"Wath that you buthin' your plathe?" he asked in a toothless hum. Before I could answer he added, "I thought you wath tryin' to give your horthe a haircut with that airplane." He laughed one of those wheezy laughs that are mostly air. He slapped his leg for emphasis.

"No, Cecil, my buddies from the flying school decided to beat-up Windy Acres today."

"Wow, with friendth like that, a fella don't need enemieth."

"You can say that again," I shrugged.

"With friendth like that, a fella don't need enemieth."

At work the next day, Eric greeted me sporting a stupid grin. "Did you get your fence fixed Farmer Brown?" he laughed.

"No, there were too many interruptions." I tried to sound angry. I was worried about my neighbours' reactions to the low flying. Eric laughed louder.

The buzz jobs continued on my next day off. It seemed that every instructor at Derry Air was teaching forced approaches to my farm when I was home. In the afternoon, there were three Piper Cherokees circling Windy Acres at one time. The pilots took turns dropping down to pasture level, aiming for the house and pulling up at the last second. I recognized Eric in one of them.

Diana Bates, one of my student customers, was an air traffic controller

in Derry Tower. I knew she was working that day. I called her and explained the problem.

"I understand," she replied. "But do you want to report them?" We both knew that an official complaint could result in a fine and possible suspension of their pilot licences.

"No, but could you pretend to report them? Maybe that will slow them down. Eric is in Tango Victor Hotel and he is headed back to the airport now."

"Sure, I'll take care of it," she said. "It'll be fun."

Later, she told me what had happened. "After Tango Victor Hotel landed, I asked the pilot-in-command to call the control tower when he got into the office. Eric phoned right away. I explained to him that his airplane had been seen flying at fence level creating a danger to people and property on the ground. I said I was writing him up.

"'Give me the guy's phone number,' Eric replied casually, 'and I'll talk to him.'

"'I can't do that,' I said. 'You'll have to work it out with Aviation Enforcement.'

"'Come on Diana,' he said a little more seriously. 'You have discretion on these things. I wasn't very low.'

"I told him that we are obliged to report all public complaints. He asked if he had been reported by a certain off-duty Derry Air flying instructor. I told him that it came from that area."

Eric called me as soon as he had hung up the tower phone. "Hi, it's Eric." His voice was not as carefree as usual. "How's it going?"

"Fine, Eric. What's up?"

"Did you call in a low-flying complaint on me?"

"No, not me," I lied. "But I should. You guys are becoming a nuisance out here."

"Well somebody in your neighbourhood did. Diana is writing me up for low flying."

"I'm not surprised. Is she writing up everyone else?"

"I don't think so. You don't sound very sympathetic."

"Well, you guys are giving me a bad name. Maybe now you'll stop targeting my place."

"Sure. Do you think you could talk to your neighbours? Maybe you could find out who called and ask them to withdraw the complaint?"

"Oh thanks for nothing." I said as sternly as possible. "After using my place for your low flying fun, you want me to spend my day off admitting to my neighbours that it was my friends who were hedge-hopping across their yards and convince them that it was a good idea?"

"Well," he said sheepishly, "yah."

"And what are you doing on your day off?"

"Updating my resume, I guess, in case you can't head off this complaint."

"Do you mind if I buzz your place in downtown Derry?"

"Okay, I get the point. I promise I won't beat-up your farm ever again. Just talk to your neighbours, please."

"What about the other instructors?"

"You'll never see them near your place. I'll take care of it, I promise."

He sounded like he meant it, but I kept the pressure on just to be sure. "Should I start with the mink breeder or the guy with the hundred prize milk cows?"

"Oh, no."

"I'll see what I can do."

There was no mink farmer and I didn't visit my dairy-farming neighbour. I phoned Diana and told her that our scheme had worked.

Eric was waiting for me when I arrived at Derry Air the next morning. "What did you find out?"

"It was the dairy farmer," I lied. "You scared his herd so badly that his automatic stable cleaner broke. He will withdraw the complaint if all the low-flying pilots will spend their days off forking manure out of the barn until he gets it fixed." I managed to keep a straight face until the end of the sentence. The sad look on Eric's face threw me into a fit of laughter.

"What's so funny?" he asked.

I was laughing so hard, I couldn't answer.

"You lying turkey! You made this up, didn't you?"

The word spread around Derry Air that I was one up on Eric.

Even though I had fabricated the complaint, it had scared the instructors enough that they didn't buzz our farm again.

Two weeks later there was a soft knocking on our door when Susan and I were finishing supper. It was Jan Vanderstock, the neighbouring dairy farmer. He stood on our porch with his cap in hand.

"Jan," I said, "come on in."

He stepped into the kitchen but declined our invitation to sit down.

"I don't vont to bodder you at dinner," he said shyly. "I yust vondered vhat happen to da airplanes?"

"Oh, don't worry, Jan," I said hastily. "They're gone for good. They won't be back."

"Never come back?"

"That's right, I promise."

"Dat's too bad," he said looking at the floor. "Vhen dey fly over, da cows give more milk. Da airplanes move da lazy herd around to better pasture."

Chapter Five

The Muldoone incident

There are two ways air traffic controllers can exit their towers: descending the stairs or repelling down a rope in an emergency. The stairways are built into the middle of the three-storey buildings. The ropes are coiled up in a cupboard in the tower cabs. They were added to all control towers after the Muldoone incident.

Bull Muldoone, called "the Pineapple" by the Derry Air staff in his absence, was a prickly customer who plowed his way through life believing that being pushy and ignorant got the best results.

The Muldoone incident started when Bull was on a return flight to Derry in his Piper Twin Comanche. He had spent an afternoon at an out-of-town racehorse track with a couple of his construction buddies. Much beer had been consumed at the track and in the airplane. The into-the-wind flight home had taken more than an hour. By the time they were approaching the Derry Airport, the bladders on all three men had reached critical pressure.

"Derry Tower, Uniform Lima Lima, 15 miles out, ah... request straight-in, Runway 24." You could hear the grimace in Muldoone's voice over the radio.

The controller on duty was Diana Bates. "Bravo Uniform Lima Lima," Diana replied. "Runway 24, wind 250 at 10, altimeter 30.09, cleared straight in, call three miles final. Traffic is two Cherokees and a Cessna 150 in the circuit."

"Lima Lima."

Muldoone pointed the nose down on his hot little twin without reducing the power. The speed topped 200 mph as he smoked toward the runway.

"Derry Tower," a solo student in the lead Cherokee said, "Tango Victor Hotel is turning base Runway 24."

"Tango Victor Hotel is cleared touch and go, Runway 24."

"Tango Victor Hotel."

Derry Air instructor Larry Buttons and a student were following in another Cherokee. Larry was too familiar with Muldoone. The loud-mouth aircraft owner liked to bully the flying school staff. Larry had been on the receiving end of Muldoone's abuse too many times. When Muldoone called in, Larry recognized an opportunity to mess up the Pineapple's approach.

"Alpha November Delta is turning base Runway 24," he said on the radio. Then he told his student to turn in tight.

"Alpha November Delta, you're number two behind the Cherokee turning final."

"With the traffic, November Delta."

"Also watch for a Twin Comanche on the straight in Runway 24, Alpha November Delta," Diana added.

"Negative contact."

"Lima Lima three miles final," Bull said quickly.

"Roger Uniform Lima Lima. Slow it up. You are number three following a Cherokee on a base leg."

"Ah... we're looking."

At that point, Larry had his student extend the flaps and slow the Cherokee down to 65 knots.

"Traffic is at your one o'clock, Lima Lima. You'll have to slow down or go around."

Muldoone spotted the second Cherokee. It was obvious that he was too close and unable to stay behind the slow-moving airplane.

"Ah... tower. This isn't working out," he said. There was desperation in his voice.

"Pull up and go around, Lima Lima. When you reach circuit height on runway heading, follow a Cessna 150 on the downwind. You are number four."

While Diana was talking, Muldoone kept coming at speed. "Ah... how about we just land behind this Cherokee on the runway?" Muldoone asked forcefully. "Maybe that other guy could do a 360 or something."

Other pilots may have gotten away with it, but Muldoone's reputation killed his chances of a compromise. He had tried to "bull" his way in the Derry Control zone before. Every Derry Airport air traffic controller, including Diana, had a reason to put Muldoone in his place. They just needed an opportunity to do it within the bounds of professional conduct.

"Negative, Lima Lima. Pull up and go around. Maintain runway heading. Advise the Cessna 150 in sight."

Muldoone pulled the nose of the Comanche up and rocketed over the middle of the airport. The extra g force brought moans from his yellow-eyed passengers. He didn't reply on the radio.

Diana called him again. "Uniform Lima Lima, advise the Cessna in sight."

Muldoone, his brain awash in beer residue, did not reply. When the Comanche reached circuit height, it banked toward the downwind. The Cessna 150 was ahead but out wide. It was being flown by a student from the flying school next to Derry Air. The instructors there were trained that large circuits generated more revenue.

"Lima, Lima. You're number three now behind the Cessna 150 on a wide downwind."

Muldoone didn't reply. He kept the two Lycomings howling and proceeded to pass the Cessna on the inside. It's possible that he never saw the airplane.

"Uniform Lima Lima, Derry Tower, do you read?"

No answer. Muldoone was concentrating on two things: flying the airplane to a landing as soon as possible and not wetting his pants.

Diana told the student in the Cessna that he was now number two behind a Twin Comanche. The student replied which confirmed that the transmitter in the tower had not failed.

"Uniform Lima Lima, Derry Tower, if you can hear this transmission, rock your wings."

At that moment, Muldoone turned on a tight base leg for the runway. His sloppy flying looked like a wing rock.

"Uniform Lima Lima," Diana said, I understand you are receiver only. You are cleared to land Runway 24, wind 250 at 10, check landing gear down."

There was no reply. Muldoone kept the speed on and the wheels up.

Diana covered all her bases. "Uniform Lima Lima, if you are experiencing any other problems, rock your wings."

Muldoone turned onto a short final leg and chopped the power to slow down. Diana probably knew that the ropey manoeuvre was just a turn, but she decided it was time to exercise the emergency crew. She hit the crash button.

"Uniform Lima Lima, Derry Tower, the crash truck is on the way."

Muldoone extended the landing gear and flaps and dropped the airplane on the runway. He stood on the brakes and turned off at the first intersection. As soon as he was off the runway, hc shut the engines down and yelled at his two fat buddies to get out of the airplane. They popped the door and squeezed out as fast as they could.

The crash truck came roaring down the taxiway. The two rescue crew were ready for everything. They were wearing full crash gear. The foam cannon mounted on the truck cab was charged and aimed at the airplane. As the truck neared the Twin Comanche, the crew saw three burly guys

Cockpit Follies

lined up along the side of the taxiway madly watering the grass and grinning in great relief. The crash chief didn't know whether to hose the airplane, the passengers or the grass. He climbed out of the truck.

"What seems to be the trouble here?" he shouted.

"Nothin'," Muldoone replied. "We're just a little short on range and high on manifold pressure." He laughed at his own joke. It was the signal for his buddies to laugh too.

"So there's nothing wrong with the airplane and everyone is all right?" the chief asked.

"The airplane's fine and so will we be in a minute," Muldoone barked over his shoulder. The three boozers continued to kill the grass.

The chief went back to the truck and reported to the tower that everything was okay. He wasn't telling Diana anything that she didn't already know. She had been watching the whole scene with binoculars.

Diana might have let the incident drop at that point but Muldoone wasn't smart enough to let her. The three belligerent beerhounds climbed back into the airplane. Muldoone made the mistake of calling for taxi instructions. "Derry Ground, Lima Lima; give me taxi to the ramp."

"Lima Lima, Derry Ground, how do you read this transmission?" Diana asked.

"I read you fine, babe, but I didn't hear my taxi instructions. We don't have all day!"

Diana could hear a beer can snapping open in the background. "Uniform Lima Lima, cleared to the ramp via Charlie, Foxtrot. When you get in, report to the control tower."

Muldoone gunned the engines down the taxiway without bothering to reply. He parked the Twin Comanche in the middle of the Derry Air ramp. Diana watched from the control tower while the three overloads exited the airplane and walked into the flying school office on their way to their truck.

Diana intended to write Muldoone up for a list of aeronautical communication violations. She knew the owner of the Twin Comanche and could soon find out his licence number but she also knew the charges would stick better if she identified him as the pilot of that flight.

Diana anticipated that Muldoone wouldn't call her so she phoned the Derry Air flight desk.

"Angel, it's Diana in the control tower. Please tell Muldoone that you have a telephone call for him."

Muldoone was walking by. Angel held out the phone and nodded in his direction. He took the call.

"Yah?"

"This is Derry Tower calling. Are you the pilot of Bravo Uniform Lima Lima?"

"What if I am?"

"I'd like to know your name and pilot licence number."

"What for?"

"I need it to complete a report that I'm filing on the trouble you were having on your last flight."

"I didn't have no trouble," Muldoone said suspiciously.

"We'll let the authorities decide that," Diana replied.

"Are you violating me?" Muldoone demanded.

"You violated yourself."

"Listen, little lady," Muldoone barked. "I've forgotten more about flying than you know."

"I believe it, sir," Diana said. "And I know quite a bit."

The boozer wasn't sure if he had just slighted himself so he changed tactics.

"Tell you what, Honey," he said winking at his buddies standing nearby. "Before you go writin' up anything, my friends and I have a couple of brews left. We'll come and talk this over."

"No thank you, sir," Diana said quickly. "Access to the control tower is deni..."

Muldoone hung up before she ended her sentence. "Come on," he said with a belch. "Let's go to the tower and see if we can straighten out that babe."

The three meatballs piled into Muldoone's crewcab construction company pickup and drove around the airport perimeter to the control tower. The entrance to the three-storey building was locked. There was an apartment-style intercom system for public access by the door. Muldoone saw the intercom and stabbed the button. Diana had watched the truck drive up. She didn't need to hear the buzzer to know who was at the door.

She pressed the reply button. "Access denied," she announced calmly. Diana was athletic, six feet tall and a university graduate. She was confident she could handle the burly, pea-brain construction owner but she was smart enough to know it was better not too. There was another controller working with her that afternoon. He nodded his approval.

Muldoone tried the door and the intercom button a few more times. There was no response. The man had spent his life getting his own way. He yelled at the tower and then charged back to his truck with his buddies in trail. He rummaged through the construction equipment piled in the pick-up box and came up smiling. In one hand he had a four-foot piece of four-by-four lumber. In the other he held a high-powered nail gun. "If she wants to be anti-social," he bellowed, "then she can rot up there forever!"

His buddies helped Muldoone carry the equipment to the base of the tower. The entrance was built to open outward. Muldoone motioned for the four-by-four to be placed on the cement pad in front of the door. He loaded the nail gun with a spike and pressed it to the top of the wooden beam.

From the tower, Diana saw the three stooges return toward the building carrying something but because of the tower balcony, she couldn't see straight down. She turned on the intercom to listen to what they were doing. At the same time, Muldoone pulled the trigger.

The blast was amplified over the speaker in the tower. Diana jabbed at the communications panel to open the direct line to the police station. The other controller dove out of his chair onto the floor.

"Police," a dispatcher answered.

"It's Derry Tower calling," Diana said quickly. "The control tower building at the airport is being attacked by three males who are armed and drunk. Request police assistance."

"Is this a joke?" the dispatcher asked.

"Bang!"

Muldoone drove spike number two into the lumber. The dispatcher could hear the shot over the telephone. "Officers are on the way," he declared. "Stay on the line. I'll get right back to you."

The dispatcher broadcast for officers to converge on the airport. In the meantime, Muldoone drove two more spikes into the beam. Diana figured that the drunken pilot was trying to shoot open the door. She thought Muldoone would be up the stairs any second but instead she saw him climb in the truck with his two buddies and drive away. She told the police dispatcher. He put out a description of the truck.

Muldoone departed the area via the back roads. He eluded the first cruiser. It was driven by Officer Roger Shirley. Roger was well known at the airport. He flew the highway patrol with Derry Air. Roger went straight to the control tower. He saw the beam across the bottom of the door. He talked to Diana over the intercom.

"I'll call Dale," Diana offered.

"Good idea," Roger replied.

Diana's husband was Dale Bates, the local tow truck operator. When Diana told him what had happened, he was at the airport in a few minutes.

Dale was six and a half feet tall and weighed a rock solid 250 pounds. He popped the piece of wood out of the concrete with an oversized pry bar. He went upstairs with Roger. While Diana continued to work the air traffic, they hatched a plot to even the score with Muldoone.

The next time the fat blowhard went flying, it was with the same two buddies and it was during one of Diana's shifts in the control tower. It was a hot summer day. They returned to see a familiar pickup truck parked beside the windsock in the middle of the infield of the Derry Airport. After he had brought the galloping Twin Comanche to a stop, Muldoone

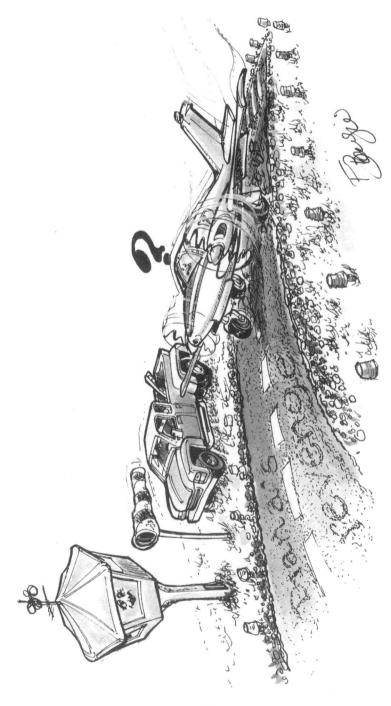

40

radioed the control tower.

"What's my truck doin' out here?" he demanded.

"Looks like its pointing into the wind," Diana replied innocently.

"Somebody's got some explainin' to do!" he roared.

She didn't reply.

Muldoone taxied to the ramp. Angel, the Derry Air receptionist, couldn't or wouldn't tell him why his truck was not where he had left it, but she offered him and his buddies a ride to the infield with Huey in the gas bowser.

When they got out there, the three beer barrels climbed into the truck. Muldoone started it up and put it in gear. It wouldn't move. Muldoone goosed the gas. The engine revved up but the truck just sat there with its wheels spinning.

"What the...?" Muldoone growled.

Dale Bates had towed the pickup to the infield and mounted both axles on wooden beams. Rev as he might, Muldoone wasn't going anywhere. Huey yelled from the cab of the tanker that he would call a tow truck. He drove back to Derry Air leaving the three overweights sweating in the summer heat.

Huey asked Angel to called Dale Bates. The tow truck operator took his time getting out to the airport. About the time Muldoone was thinking about walking back to the ramp, Dale arrived in his tow truck.

"What took you so long?" Muldoone roared.

Dale pointed to the sign on the side of his truck, "23-hour towing".

"Your call came in during my one hour off," he explained, holding a straight face.

"Well, hurry up. I don't have all day," Muldoone boomed.

"I do," Dale replied.

He slowly and deliberately took his time hooking the front of the pick-up to the tow crane. He lifted the front end enough to remove the wooden beam underneath. Then he let the truck down and drove around behind it. He lifted the rear of the truck up and pulled out the beam. Muldoone was ready to jump in and roar away as soon as the rear was released but Dale had other ideas. He tossed the beam into the back of the tow truck, hopped in and drove away with the pickup on the hook. He left Muldoone and his buddies waddling after him, shaking their fists.

"Come back you jerk!" Muldoone yelled.

The three stranded amigos had no choice but to hoof it through a kilometre of heat and grass back to Derry Air. They were about halfway when a police cruiser came out to meet them. Officer Roger Shirley offered them a ride.

Muldoone was fuming. "Wait 'til I get my hands on that idiot truck driver!" he exclaimed. He climbed into the cruiser and slammed the door.

When the other two got in, Roger activated the locks.

"You won't have to wait long," Roger said. "He's expecting us at his yard. His wife was the air traffic controller working the day you fired the beam into the door. I'll take you to him and if there is anything left of you when he's finished, I want to talk to you about a weapons violation."

Chapter Six

Inspector Crusty

Inspector Kennedy descended on Derry Air for a base inspection. He tried to sneak up on us but we knew he was coming. The government was the only operator in the area that could afford Beechcraft Barons.

I was in the chief flying instructor's office with Eric when we heard Kennedy call the Derry Control Tower on the office radio monitor. He landed and called for taxi clearance "to the ramp" to disguise which of the two flying schools on the field was his destination. He taxied in and shut down halfway between the two hangars. The Baron was camouflaged in plain white paint and a thin red stripe to make it look inconspicuous but we had known he was coming to Derry Air for three days.

Angel had friends among the support personnel in the government aviation office. She had received a phone call earlier that week.

"Hi, it's Mildred at Aviation. I just called to find out if you have an instructor candidate up for a flight test on Thursday? Kennedy has booked the Baron out to Derry for the day and I don't have a record of a flight test. I just wondered if I'd missed something?"

"No. No flight test here," Angel replied.

"Oh well. Sorry to bother you. He must be flying over there for something else. Have a good day."

Most government aviation inspectors were reasonable, friendly and helpful. They were usually former members of the industry who continued to contribute positively to aviation by joining the government. Kennedy seemed to go out of his way to be unreasonable, unfriendly and unhelpful. He had been an inspector so long that no one could recall where he came from. Everyone wished that he would go back.

Eric and I hid in the CFI office and watched Kennedy strut purposefully across the ramp toward Derry Air. He was wearing a rumpled gray government suit. A scowl was chiseled into his granite face. He walked through the door and was greeted by a pile of aircraft journey log books stacked on the flight desk beside Angel. He nodded a greeting to her. Angel nodded back.

It was interesting to see how each Derry Air supervisor reacted to the crusty inspector's visit. It wouldn't have mattered to Angel if we hadn't heard about the inspection. She was a fanatical bookkeeper. She ruled Derry Air while squatting on her stool and the aircraft journey and technical logs were part of her domain. They were kept up-to-date after every flight. Her encyclopedic mind knew the times to the next inspection on all ten aircraft including the hours to go on the engine overhaul and expiry on the calendar components without looking in the logs. She ragged Darcy Philips, the chief mechanic, so that Derry Air never missed scheduled maintenance on the fleet. Her pursuit of perfection was a perfect way to combat Kennedy's unreasonable enforcement of regulations.

"I'm here on a base inspection," Kennedy said to Angel.

The receptionist nodded again, this time toward the books. She never wasted words with anyone else so she wasn't going to start jawing with Kennedy. He started looking through the logs. Occasionally he made notes on a clipboard. He finished by saying, "I'll be inspecting these aircraft this afternoon."

"Going to Windsor?" Angel asked in her monotone voice.

"I beg your pardon?"

"Are you going to Windsor?" Angel repeated without further explanation.

"No."

"Then you won't be inspecting Tango Victor Hotel."

Kennedy realized what she was telling him. "It's convenient that an aircraft will be leaving during a base inspection," he said.

"It's called revenue," Angel said flatly. "If I can get rid of the rest of them, I will."

It was score "one" for Angel.

Kennedy ignored the comeback and started looking through the daily flight sheets on the counter. He stopped three pages back. "There is an incomplete entry on Tuesday," he said sternly. "These records are to be filled in within 24 hours."

Angel didn't need to look at it. "The airplane is on a trip. When it returns, I'll complete the entry."

(Angel 2, Kennedy 0)

The inspector changed the subject. "Where are your Pilot Training Records?"

Angel motioned to the bookshelves of student records at the end of the lounge. This was Eric's cue to make an appearance. He stepped to the door of his office. "Good morning sir," he said with a forced cheerfulness.

"How are you today?"

I was listening from my hiding place behind the door. I could tell from his voice that the normally jolly CFI was uptight. Kennedy only nodded in reply to the greeting. He immediately began flipping through the training records at random. Eric stood there with his arms folded.

"There are students here," Kennedy said, holding out one of the booklets for Eric to see, "who were sent on their first solo flight without completing all the exercises between one and eighteen."

Eric took the book and turned through the four pages of entries. "All of the exercises have been covered according to this," he said.

"Show me number seventeen," Kennedy demanded triumphantly.

"The circuit? It was covered many times with takeoffs and landings," Eric replied. He pointed to a string of entries showing "16-18".

"The department does not accept the 'dash' as a proper record of events," Kennedy said. He stuck out his jaw to emphasize his authority.

The CFI removed a pen from his shirt pocket and wrote "17" in the pilot training record several times. He handed the book back to Kennedy.

"You are falsifying a federal document," Kennedy declared.

"And you are making a mountain out of mole hill," Eric shot back. "What else can I do for you?"

He made a note on his clipboard. "See that your instructors learn how to make proper entries."

"Yes sir," Eric replied through clenched teeth.

"I want to inspect your library."

I realized too late that I should have escaped to the hangar. I hid behind the door hoping he didn't see me. Eric ushered the inspector into his office and pointed to the collection of reference manuals on the bookshelves. Kennedy checked the required books against a list on his clipboard.

"Your Airmen's Information Publication is missing," he declared. He marked it down.

"One of the flying instructors borrowed it to study for a Class 2 written exam," Eric said.

"You are in violation of your Operating Certificate because you have an incomplete library."

I could see Eric's neck turning red. "It's a reference library," Eric said. "It's a reference book. It's being referenced." The easy-going CFI was getting fed up.

"It's missing," Kennedy replied. He was not yielding. "It's a discrepancy."

"Are you telling me that a reference library is only in compliance when none of the books are being read?"

"I'm telling you the library is incomplete."

With that he turned and looked at the greaseboard list of instructor training and licence expiring dates. "You have a staff member working on an expired medical," he said almost immediately.

I looked at the board. The name beside the expired medical was mine. Yet I had had a recent medical. Eric glanced at the board. "No, I have a board that isn't up-to-date," he said stiffly.

"What good is the board if it isn't maintained?"

"Having the board is a requirement of your office," Eric growled. "So we have a board. Having an up-to-date medical is the instructor's responsibility."

"I'll check the records when I get back to the office," Kennedy threatened. "If I find..."

Eric interrupted him. "You don't have to," he said. "The instructor is sitting behind you."

Kennedy turned around. I grinned sheepishly.

"Show me your pilot documents," he demanded. He held out his hand impatiently.

I pulled my wallet out and extracted my pilot licence and medical. Kennedy glanced at them quickly. He shoved them back in my direction.

"Your licence is invalid," he declared and then made a note on his clipboard.

I looked at the document. I couldn't see anything wrong. Kennedy stabbed a triumphant finger at it.

"You haven't signed it. You're instructing illegally."

His nitpicking sent Eric off the deep end. "The regs require a licence!" He was close to yelling now. "Nowhere does it say it has to be signed!"

Kennedy stayed calm but sounded just as determined. "The licence is not a licence if it isn't signed."

"That's bureaucratic bull!" Eric barked. His face turned red. "Stop bothering us with your officious nonsense and go chase pilots flying without licences!"

"You'll be receiving a letter," Kennedy said sternly. He walked out of the office, into the lounge and through the door to the hangar.

Eric paced back and forth and steamed. I stood there without saying anything. When he finally spoke, he said, "I swear to myself that I'm not going to lose my temper but every time he comes, I do. The guy brings out my worst."

"Come on," I said. "I'll buy you a coffee."

"Make it a scotch."

In the hangar, Derry Air chief mechanic Darcy Philips handled the base inspection differently. His crew had spent the last three days finishing up their work, pushing the airplanes out to the tie-down area and cleaning up the shop. Everything that could be lifted was moved into the parts room. It was filled to the rafters and padlocked. A sign was hung on the door that said, "Quarantine". This meant that everything stacked behind the sign did not have to be documented as airworthy.

When they were done, Darcy gave the mechanics the day off. Kennedy walked through the door to a shop that was empty except for Darcy sitting in his office with his feet up.

"He looked mad already," Darcy told Eric and me later. "'Hi, Igor,' I said. 'How's it going?'

"He looked around. 'Where is everything?' he asked.

"'All done,' I said. 'So I gave the boys the day off.'

"I knew that wouldn't stop him checking all the maintenance logs with a magnifying glass, so I threw in my diversionary tactic.

"'I guess you had a little problem with the Baron on the way over,' I said.

"'No. I didn't have a problem.'

"'Oh? How come there's a pool of oil collecting under the left engine?'

"'What oil?'

"'Come on out and I'll show you,' I replied. 'We can do this inspection after.'"

Darcy said that they went out to the ramp and sure enough, oil was dripping out of the Baron's left engine and forming a growing puddle on the ground. He was grinning while he told us.

"I offered to take the cowling off to check it out. He agreed. I told him that I'd have to see the aircraft log books first.

"'Why is that?' he asked.

"'I don't work on an aircraft unless the log books are in order,' I replied." Darcy's grin was getting wider as he related the conversation.

"'This is a government aircraft,' he said." Darcy mimicked Kennedy's pompous voice. "'The paperwork is fine.'

"'Sure and the airplane never leaks oil,' I replied.

"He dug the logs out of the cabin. He was right. They were up-to-date. Can you believe that ten-year-old airplane has only 1,200 hours on it? That's criminal under-utilization. Anyway, I dropped the cowlings and there was oil everywhere. I suggested that he run the engine so I could see where the leak was coming from.

"'I'll have to see your pilot licence first,' I said." Darcy laughed. "That really ticked him off.

"'A pilot licence is not required for an engine run-up,' he replied.

"'No, but competency is. A pilot licence is proof of competency.'

"'I flew this airplane here!' he declared.

"'Well, if you did it without a pilot licence, then I guess you're in big trouble, aren't you?'

"I couldn't believe it." Darcy was laughing. "Old granite cheeks actually showed me his licence."

"Was it valid?" Eric asked with a chuckle.

"I don't know. How do you tell?"

"It has to be signed," I offered.

"I didn't look but I know it's covered with oily fingerprints now. Anyway, Igor started the left engine. As soon as he applied power, the line running to the oil cooler blew off. The blast from the propeller whipped it around. Oil spewed everywhere. I gave him the shutdown sign," Darcy said drawing his hand across his throat.

"I told him that we were facing major work." Darcy was still laughing. "He believed me. He even helped me pull the airplane up to the hangar. I could have used the tractor but I wanted to see him do real work. I suggested if he helped me, we might get it fixed before I went home at four o'clock." Darcy laughed louder at the suggestion that he quit at four. "He said he'd help. I offered him a pair of coveralls.

"I had him spray the engine down with varsol. He did a good job. Very thorough. He passed me wrenches while I removed the oil line. There was nothing wrong with it. It had just been loose but I suggested that I change it. He agreed. I had him sign a triplicate work order. He liked that.

"When the lunch truck came, he joined me for a break. We talked. He said that he had done his pilot training in the air force and had gone straight into the government. He had never worked on an airplane before."

"We wondered what had happened to him," Eric said, "but I didn't want to go out there to find out. I figured it was better to have him bugging you than me. Now I wish I had seen him working in coveralls."

"Hey, he was having fun. I let him put the new oil line on. We pushed the airplane out and he ran it up to check for leaks. It was fine. He helped me reinstall the cowlings and then we washed the oil off the whole airplane. We're buddies now.

"When we were done, it was three o'clock. He thanked me and left."

"I'm impressed," Eric said. "You were lucky the oil line was loose. How did you happened to spot the oil on the ground all the way across the ramp?"

"Hey. Good flying school maintenance doesn't run on luck. I loosened the oil line when Inspector Crusty was in here ragging you."

Chapter Seven

IFR renewal

My first multi-engine instrument rating renewal was due at the end of the month. I wasn't looking forward to it. There had been no chance for hands-on IFR practice. I was rusty. Derry Air boss Stingy Mingy didn't offer free training time to his instructing staff and I still owed money on my initial training six months ago.

Dutch was helpful. The Derry Air ground instructor wrung me out "in za box". In exchange, I taught one of his ground school classes. Henry, one of the other instructors, road shotgun with me on one practice flight up and down the Derry Airport localizer for Runway 06/24.

I booked the flight test in Toronto and flew the Derry Air Twin Comanche over on the appointed day. I was nervous about the test but found consolation in the good weather. It was cool but the air was calm and clear except for a thin layer of broken clouds at 5,000. I flew the ILS straight in on Runway 06 Right at Toronto. Everything on the old Piper was working fine. My confidence was on the rise.

I shut the airplane down in front of the government hangar. I walked to the office, opened the door and came face-to-face with Inspector Kennedy. He looked as miserable as ever. My jaw dropped. I stood there with my mouth open.

"What are you doing here?" he barked.

"I... ah... thought I had an IFR flight test this morning," I answered tentatively.

"You should have called first," Kennedy declared.

"Ah, your office has only been open half an hour," I said. "Is there a problem?"

"Didn't you check the weather?" he asked sharply.

"Yes, sir," I replied. I looked out the window to indicate that was all that was necessary on such a clear day.

"Check again," he growled, pushing a weather printout across the counter.

I looked at the sequence for Toronto. It didn't tell me anything I didn't know. The ceiling was 5,000 feet thin broken, the visibility was 15 miles plus and the wind was calm.

"It looks fine to me," I said in a neutral, non-committing tone.

"Is your Twin Comanche equipped and certified for flights into known icing?" he asked. He knew it wasn't.

"No sir."

"Then your flight test is cancelled."

"I... I... don't understand, sir," I sputtered. "The weather is fine. I just flew in it."

"The freezing level is at 4,000 feet," Kennedy explained loudly and slowly. He jabbed a finger at the weather report on the counter as he spoke, "Which means there is icing in clouds that are at 5,000 feet so we don't fly."

If it had been anyone else, I would have assumed it was a joke but in past encounters, this man had demonstrated that he had no sense of humour. I considered pleading with him. After all, I had taken a half-day off work and spent two days' pay to arrive at his counter. There was no reason he could not fly with me under 5,000 feet. He stood there with a lockjaw look on his face. I thought of asking him why I had not crashed in such horrible weather on the way over but I stopped myself. If he flew with me after such a sarcastic remark, I would surely fail. There was nothing to do but turn around and fly back to Derry. So I did. I mentally burned Kennedy in effigy all the way home.

When I walked into the flying school office, Eric knew I was back too soon.

"What happened?" he asked.

"I think I just paid for the way we treated Kennedy during his base inspection," I said. I told him about my encounter with Inspector Crusty.

"That's crazy," Eric said. "What was Kennedy doing in the IFR section? He's an instructor standards inspector."

"I don't know. Gunning for Derry Air, I guess."

"Did you reschedule?"

"No, I wanted to see when I could spring me and the airplane again."

"Let me make a call," Eric said, walking over to the counter phone. "I know the chief IFR inspector."

I waited while Eric called Toronto. "Hello, Les? Hi, it's Daedalus at Derry."

"Fine, thank you. Say, I'm going to need a six-month extension on one of my instructor's IFR Ratings."

It was a strange request. Weather delays qualified IFR candidates for a maximum 30-day extension.

"Well, he's due at the end of the month but apparently your inspectors have stopped doing instrument tests in the fall."

"I'm talking about today: 5,000 thin broken and he was refused a renewal ride in a Twin Comanche. I don't mind as long as you are good for extensions into the summer for all my staff."

"Kennedy; every pilot's friend."

"Okay, thanks. I'll wait for your call."

Eric hung up the telephone. He was smiling. "He's going to look into it and call me back."

"I like the way you handled that," I said sarcastically. "I'll either get an instrument renewal today or never."

"Hold the applause until we see what happens."

Chief Inspector Les Appleseed called Eric back that afternoon. I was flying with a student. The CFI was sporting a huge grin when I came back.

"You're not going to believe this," he said. "You have an IFR flight test, here, tomorrow, in the morning, at 10:30. I've made the airplane available and I'll fly with your student."

"Wow. How did you swing that?"

"Les wouldn't or couldn't admit that you were being jerked around by Kennedy but his actions spoke louder than words. He's flying Inspector Kennedy here to our front door tomorrow morning. He's doing it as part of a training flight with another inspector in one of their King Airs."

All the colour drained from my face. "Kennedy?" I moaned. "I'll fail for sure."

"Don't bet on it," Eric said. "Kennedy knows that Appleseed has his number. If he tries to hassle you again, he'll be in big trouble. Making him come here tomorrow at your convenience is already a form of reprimand." Eric was excited.

"That's what I'm afraid of," I said. "You're happy but you don't have to fly with the sorry man."

"Don't worry," he said, patting me on the shoulder. "Just do your best."

The next morning dawned to moderate snow flurries blowing off Lake Ontario. I was relieved to know the flight test would be cancelled. Visibility was one to two miles in the white stuff. All our VFR lessons were postponed.

"Shall I call for another IFR booking," I asked Eric, "or do you want to do that with your friend Appleseed?"

"Let's wait to see if they show up first. The snow is falling from high cloud. It's good weather for an instrument test."

A few minutes later we could hear "Inspector One" on the office monitor calling Derry Tower. He was reporting on the localizer for the ILS approach to Derry Runway 06. The King Air landed and taxied to the Derry Air ramp in a swirl of snow. I thought it was pretty stupid to fly to Derry just to tell me that my second test was cancelled. At least this time it wasn't my money being wasted. The left engine on the turboprop was shut down and the airstair door swung down. Inspector Kennedy climbed out. He turned around and closed the door. The engine was restarted and the airplane taxied back toward the runways. Just seeing the man made my mouth dry and knotted my stomach. I waited by the flight desk while he made tracks through the snow to the door. Eric hid in his office.

"Good morning sir," I said with forced cheerfulness.

"Are you ready to go?" he asked. His look was at full stern but some of the bark had gone out of his speech. I couldn't believe that he would consider doing the flight test.

"Ah... no... sir," I said haltingly. "I didn't know what you wanted to do... ah... in this weather."

"File an IFR flight plan for approaches at Derry with a suitable alternate," he said. "I'll hit the washroom and we'll go."

By the time he had come back, I was warming up to the fact that we were going flying. "We're filed," I said, "but I haven't checked over the airplane or swept the snow off it."

"Well, let's go," he said. "I'll help you."

I gathered up my flight bag, the aircraft log book and a broom. Kennedy took the broom from me and held open the door. We walked to the airplane in silence. I wanted to say something about it being a great day for a flight but I bit my tongue instead.

He swept the loose snow off the airplane while I did a walkaround inspection. "All set?" he asked when we were done.

"Yes sir."

"I'll take the broom back to the office while you settle in the left seat." His tone wasn't friendly but he was sounding more helpful than ever before.

When Kennedy climbed into the airplane beside me, he said, "What would you do if there was smoke coming out from behind the instrument panel?"

"I'd get out," I replied without thinking.

His face went to maximum frown. I realized that he was testing the emergency portion of the examination.

"Oh, if you mean in the air," I added quickly, "I'd declare an emergency and turn the master switch off to see if the smoke decreased."

"And if it did decrease and you were flying in IFR conditions?"

"I'd shut all the electrics off and turn the master back on. If the smoke did not reoccur, I'd turn on minimum electrics one at a time starting with the nav/com. If I could get it to work without smoking, I'd get a clearance to the nearest suitable IFR airport for an approach."

"Go ahead and start it up," he said. He seemed satisfied with my second answer. "It looks like we'll be using Runway 06. Plan on flying straight into an ILS approach to Runway 24."

"Yes sir."

I relayed the approach request to the ground controller and asked for taxi instructions. He cleared me to Runway 06 and said my clearance was on request. I taxied out through the snow, checking the instruments as I went. After I had done the run-up check, the controller called back.

"I've got the King Air holding for an approach on 06. I'll give you a clearance to hold for Runway 24 and you two can take turns holding and approaching."

I looked at Kennedy. He nodded an affirmative. "Okay," I said.

"ATC clears Yankee Alpha Victor to the Stelco fix to hold northeast inbound on the localizer, maintain 2,500, expect approach clearance at 16:20."

I read the clearance back.

"Readback correct. Yankee Alpha Victor is cleared for takeoff Runway 06. Call entering the hold."

I took off. The visibility on the ground was over a mile but it dropped as soon as we started climbing off the runway. I had brought along a hood but we weren't going to need it. It was like flying in the winter scene in a paperweight shaken by an overactive five-year-old high on sugar at Christmas. It was the first time I had flown as pilot-in-command in actual instrument conditions. I struggled to climb straight. I found flying on instruments without a hood distracting.

I flew away from the airport on the runway localizer. When I called entering the hold, the controller gave the government King Air an approach clearance for Runway 06 and an overshoot clearance to hold on the Stelco fix above us. When the King Air pilot called on the missed approach, he was given a vector off the localizer and we were cleared for an approach.

Kennedy took over the radio communications and copied an overshoot clearance. I was busy. The activity helped my nervousness but I was still uptight. Kennedy left me alone to sink or swim. I could see out of the corner of my eye that he was watching for a build-up of ice on the wing. There wasn't any. I overcontrolled a bit but managed to nail the localizer on the backcourse approach. It helped to be flying in my own backyard.

We flew an overshoot into a hold at the Derry beacon. The King Air pilots did an approach to Runway 24 to a full stop landing. After they were down, we were cleared for the approach on 06. Kennedy told the controller that it would be a full stop.

He was making this test a cakewalk, I thought to myself. He was probably too chicken to do a real test in bad weather.

"You're cleared for the ILS for Runway 06," Kennedy said to me. I read it back. He continued to stare at the wing.

I called by the beacon outbound in a racetrack entry to the approach. I did a pre-landing check, extended the gear and flaps and set up a descent. When I was levelling off and turning to intercept the localizer inbound, Kennedy pulled the mixture on the right engine.

"Simulated engine failure," he declared.

The localizer needle was centring nicely when I added power on the left engine. The airplane swung right and lost height. I cranked left, applied full power and snapped the gear up. Before I could recapture the localizer, Kennedy shut off both my ILS receivers. "Simulated ILS failure," he said. I had not been watching the ADF. He knew it.

It was the end of the cakewalk. I turned parallel to the inbound course. The ADF needle read ten degrees left of the nose. I turned toward it against the torque of the howling left engine. The ADF needle tracked left. We were passing the beacon inbound already. I was too high and to the right. I reduced the power. The airplane swung left. The approach was going to hell in a handbasket. I made no attempt to do an engine-out check or final check. I included the windshield in my scan hoping a landmark would bail me out. There was nothing to see but snow. The ADF needle read five degrees off the tail but I was flying 30 degrees off the runway heading. I had flown too far left. I turned to the inbound course and checked my stopwatch. It wasn't running.

The airplane was reaching the minimum altitude. I added power. We swung right. Dark shapes were appearing on the ground. I could see farmhouses but no airport. I thought that the approach time must have been up. I decided that I had blown the ride when a familiar house came into view. It was Angel's parent's place. I knew exactly where it was. We were a half-mile left and just short of the runway. I cranked the Comanche right and glimpsed an approach light. The runway came into view. It was headed 30 degrees to the left. I turned and chopped the power. The gear-up horn sounded. I could feel my face turn red. I lowered the undercarriage just in time to flare out and touch down. I braked and turned off the runway.

The sweat was dripping off me. The controller cleared us to the ramp. Kennedy acknowledged but said nothing to me. We taxied in silence.

I had salvaged the approach but I had blown the ride. I parked beside the King Air in front of the flying school and shut the engines down.

"A substandard performance," Kennedy declared.

"Yes sir," I replied.

He opened the door and climbed out. I quickly gathered up my stuff and followed him across the ramp.

Inside, Eric was sitting with two men who were laughing at his jokes.

"Well how did you make out?" the biggest man asked. His voice was loud

Cockpit Follies

but jovial. I guessed that he was Chief Inspector Les Appleseed.

Kennedy looked at me and then at his boss. "Not very well," he said weakly.

"What do you mean?" Appleseed boomed, still smiling. "Either he passed or he didn't. If he passed, he owes us all a round of coffee. If he failed, you can buy the coffee and we'll drink it while you fly with him again until he gets it right."

"He passed," Kennedy said.

Chapter Eight

The Phantom

One night a thief stole a Piper Warrior from a flying school in a town not far from Derry. It was someone's idea of a lark. The next morning, the radio stations and newspapers in the area received a brief phone call.

"The Phantom has struck. You'll find the missing airplane in a field on County Road Seven." The voice was muffled and mocking. "Where will the Phantom strike next?" it asked.

The media phoned the police but not before they dispatched reporters to the scene. They found a Warrior parked in a cut hay field. It was not damaged and nothing was missing from it. Pictures of the airplane ran on the front page of the local newspapers. The radio stations reported receiving "The Phantom's" phone call. After the Warrior had been checked over, a pilot from the school flew it out of the field.

Derry Air owner Irving Mingy's reactions to the incident were true to his military background. He mobilized a staff tour that morning to review the flying school's security measures. Some of the locking rods on the doors of the World War II hangar that housed Derry Air were found to be bent or broken. He ordered the aircraft mechanics to fix them. He also had them build a lockable cupboard to house the aircraft keys instead of having them piled on the front counter at the end of the day. He had Angel draw up a "Last one out" list. That person was responsible for locking the office and hangar doors. He spent extra time reviewing these procedures with the linecrew, Huey, Duey, Louey and Crazy Jim.

In two weeks the Phantom struck again. This time he stole a Cessna 172 from another airport in the area. Apparently he took the airplane in the dark, flew around until first light and then landed in a smooth field. He escaped from the area and phoned the media.

Using a muffled, spooky voice, he said, "The Ph-a-an-tom-om ha-a-as stru-u-uck agai-ai-ain."

He told the media where the airplane could be found. It was sitting there undamaged and later was flown out of the field. The story fell to the inside of the newspapers but at Derry Air, the Phantom was the hot topic of conversation.

"It must be somebody local," Eric Daedalus said that morning over coffee.

"How about Huey, Duey and Louey?" I suggested. "They love a prank."

"Naw," Henry Rains replied. "I've flown with Huey. His eyes were closed with fear the whole time we were up. Duey is the one who taxied a Cherokee through the hangar door when it was closed because he thought the throttle worked like toe brakes: 'in for stop'. Louey might be smart enough to fly but he's afraid of heights."

"I guess it could be any pilot in this area."

The next week, the Phantom helped himself to a Cherokee from Derry Air. He was able to swing in an unpinned door and squeeze through the crack. The early linecrew shift of Huey, Duey and Louey were greeted that morning at the open hangar doors by three local news reporters.

"Did you know that one of your aircraft was stolen?" the first reporter asked.

"Yes," Louey said.

"What can you tell us about it?" the second reporter asked.

"Nothing," Louey replied.

"You just said you knew about it," the third said.

Louey pointed at the first reporter. "He just told me. If you want to know more, ask him." It was a typical Louey conversation.

The thief had taken the airplane from Derry Air during the night and had landed it on a sod farm outside of town at first light. The morning radio broadcasts carried the story. "I could have done it myself," Louey was quoted as saying. "This hangar door swings open with a good push from the outside."

The afternoon paper carried a photo of the airplane in the field and one of Duey showing the reporters how a pen knife will unlock any Piper door and turn on the ignition.

Mingy was furious. The linecrew had not told him that they had lost their keys long ago. They always left the locking pins on a certain door out of the holes so they could break in every morning. He was ready to fire them but Dutch, the ground school instructor, intervened.

"You tink you know it all," the firey Dutchman said to Mingy. "If you're so smart, you'd know dat da doors heave. Da lock von't open all da time. Da boys lose dere keys 'cause dey never vork."

"They should have told me," Mingy fumed.

"Ya and you vould fix da lock. Next mont' it don't vork."

"So now we lose a Cherokee."

"Lose, schmoose. You lose nutting. Da airplane sit out dere fine and you get Derry Air in da newspaper. Use your head and run ad dat says

'Learn to fly vit da Phantom'."

The money making possiblities of Dutch's last suggestion made Mingy stop and think. The Dutchman wasn't finished.

"If you vere as smart as da linecrew, you vould have left a Cherokee outside every night vit the key and gas in. Dat vay you know dere be no damage to da place."

The Dutchman's logic prevailed. Huey, Duey and Loucy stayed employed. Mingy drove the chief mechanic Darcy and chief pilot Eric to the sod field. The airplane was not damaged and the sod was perfectly smooth. Eric flew the Cherokee back to the airport. News coverage of the incident was buried in the community pages.

That afternoon Officer Roger Shirley came to Derry Air with a tape recorder. I knew Roger as the policeman who flew in the back seat of the Derry Air Cessna 172 on the highway patrol. Eric asked me to join him and the friendly cop in Mingy's office. They closed the door behind me.

"I'm going to play a tape of the Phantom's phone call to a radio station," Roger said. "Tell me if you recognize who this is."

The voice was muffled and sounding artificially spooky but the speaker's identity was unmistakable. It was Ray Tragunno, a former Derry Air instructor who hung around the flying school on rainy days swapping stories with the flying staff. Ray had landed a job as a second officer on Boeing 747s with Major Airlines. He was the only one with a voice that low. He had wanted to be an airline pilot so badly that he had trained his voice to come from his boots.

I looked at Eric. His face told me that he also knew and now he knew that I knew. I didn't want to say anything. If Ray was charged with stealing airplanes, it would be the end of his airline career. I knew he was hard up for things to do. The airline job came with too much time off but I couldn't believe he'd play "The Phantom". He could rent the aircraft anytime.

"He knows," Eric said to Roger.

Roger looked at me. "The tape is inadmissible in court," he said. "If you know who this is, Eric has a plan to stop him without getting the guy in trouble."

I hesitated.

"So far this guy is up for public mischief," Roger continued. "I don't care if we ever catch him. In fact, we're happy that he's diverting the media from the important police work but Eric wants to stop him before he gets into real trouble."

"It sounds like Ray Tragunno," I said.

Eric agreed.

"What are you going to do?" I asked.

"Scare him so badly that he won't do it again," Eric replied.

Eric and Darcy had a plan. The chief mechanic's hobby was flying radio controlled model aircraft. With help from Fritz in the Derry Air avionics shop, he rigged one of the Derry Air Cherokee 140s and waited for Ray to show up on a bad weather day.

It rained on Thursday. Ray sauntered in about 10:30 and joined the instructors sitting around the coffeemaker. "Hi guys. What's up?" he asked. It was the same voice.

We all looked to Eric to carry the conversation. "Not much today, Ray," Eric said. "Even the Phantom isn't flying."

"Yah, what's with this Phantom thing, anyway?"

"Beats us," Eric replied. "But the guy's got us worried."

"Why is that? He's not hurting anything is he?"

"Not yet but his pranks have coincided with Irv's new policy of allowing rentals before regular hours. We occasionally leave an aircraft on the ramp with fuel and keys overnight. We're afraid it'll make it too easy for the Phantom to strike here again."

"Well, if he's just having fun," Ray said casually, "it's no big deal."

"It is to Irv. You know how fanatical he is about making money. If the airplane is gone when the customer gets here, we lose the revenue."

"Oh yah. That would really bug the old money bags," Ray said with a big grin.

"If the weather clears up, which it should," Eric continued, "Tango Victor Hotel will be parked out there tonight."

"Well, tell the customer to read the morning paper. It will tell him where the Phantom left the airplane."

The rest of us looked at the floor.

The conversation shifted to other things. The trap had been set. It was just a question of whether the Phantom would take the bait.

That night, the weather cleared as forecasted. The Cherokee was parked on our ramp with full fuel and the key in the ignition.

Darcy lived within sight of the airport. He went to bed with his model control box on the night table. It was rigged to buzz if the Cherokee was started. He woke up at first light. The control box was silent.

"I was just getting ready to go to work," Darcy told us later, "when the buzzer went off. I hotfooted it outside. A few minutes later, I could see the Cherokee taking off. I thought the Phantom was getting lazy, waiting until seven thirty to do his stuff."

Darcy telephoned Roger Shirley, who lived not far away. Then he started manipulating the control box. He had rigged one of the model radio channels to the airplane's ignition.

"When he was climbing through 400 feet, I killed the engine. He set up a glide. I restored his power at 200 feet. I let him climb to 500 feet and killed it again."

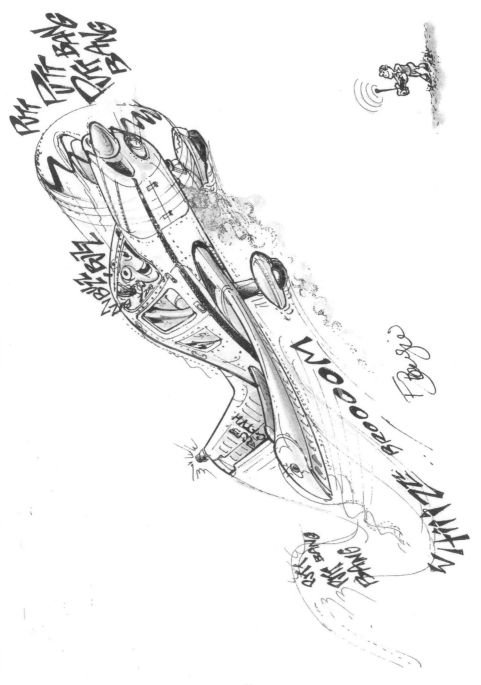

Cockpit Follies

Darcy forced the aircraft to step climb through a series of engine cuts and restarts. "I blipped his stall horn on a few times. The result was some jerky flying."

When the pilot started a left turn, Darcy fired off a smoke bomb that was planted in the engine compartment. "He was almost over my house. I could hear the whiz and the bang. Then the smoke poured out of the cowling. He looked like the Red Baron on his last flight."

As the pilot was struggling to turn the airplane back to the airport, Darcy activated the winglever autopilot which had been set to turn the airplane to the right. "The guy was all over the sky. Every time he forced the airplane to roll left, I shut the autopilot off. The airplane would snap the other way. When he managed to turn the airplane on final for a landing, I gave him the whole works: engine cuts, stall horn and autopilot roll."

After a rough landing, the Cherokee taxied onto the Derry Air ramp. Roger was waiting for him in a police cruiser. The engine was shut down. Roger walked around to the door side. When the Phantom stepped out, Roger was ready to arrest him for the final scare except it wasn't Ray. The airplane had been booked by a regular customer for eight o'clock. The guy had come early to plan his flight, saw that the airplane was ready to go and helped himself. When he crawled out of the Cherokee, he was shaking so badly, Roger had to help him step down to the asphalt. He dropped to his knees and kissed the ground.

Chapter Nine

Edgar Edgar

Edgar Edgar was Derry Air's oldest customer. He had learned to fly in the 1930s in a Taylor Cub. Once a month he rented a flying school Cherokee 140 for an hour. His appearances were like clockwork. When the government pension cheques were out, Angel got a call from Edgar to book a flight.

The little old man never flew with passengers. "My friends are either lame or gone," he shouted to me one day at the flight desk.

"That's too bad," I replied.

"Eh?"

"That's too bad!" I yelled.

"No it's not. The lame ones are sick in the head." He twirled his finger around his right ear for emphasis. "All they do is sit around and talk about what ails them."

Derry Air chief instructor Eric Daedalus wasn't concerned with Edgar being too old to fly.

"Some day he'll have to give it up but he seems to have all his marbles and knows how to use them."

I was booked with Edgar for his annual proficiency check.

"Just make sure he can still fly," Eric said, "but don't worry too much about his technique."

"What do you mean?"

"You'll see."

On the appointed day, the little octogenarian arrived with his cushion. "Ready to go sonny?" he barked.

"Yes sir!" I replied.

We went out to the airplane. I walked around with Edgar while he checked the fuel and oil levels. He started to climb into the airplane without looking at anything else.

"How about draining a fuel sample?" I suggested loudly.

"What for?" he frowned.

"To check for water, other contaminants and colour," I shouted.

He sat down in the airplane. "The engine was still warm," he said. "If the fuel was bad, the airplane wouldn't be here. It would have crashed and we'd be taking another one. It didn't crash and it hasn't been refuelled."

He was right. He did up his seat belt. I climbed in.

Edgar moved the pilot seat all the way up so he could reach the rudder pedals. He turned the master switch and fuel pump on and pushed in the mixture control. Then he cracked the throttle open and turned the key. The engine started. He turned on the radio, held the microphone a foot away from his mouth and yelled. "Alpha Nan Dog for taxi instructions!"

The ground controller was obviously familiar with Edgar and the old phonetic alphabet.

"Sounds like Edgar in Alpha November Delta," the controller replied. "Good morning."

Edgar had the volume cranked so high, the cheap cabin speaker was bouncing in the ceiling.

"Runway 24 for you, wind 240 at 10, altimeter 30.09, taxi Foxtrot, Charlie to hold short of 24. Call the tower when ready."

Edgar leaned forward to see over the instrument panel. Then he released the brakes and started taxiing without a reply. He wandered back and forth. I thought he was overcontrolling until I realized he was using an old Cub pilot trick to see better over the nose. Beside the runway, he ran the engine up long enough to check the individual magnetos. He wasn't wasting any time on details. I scanned the cockpit. Everything seemed set to go except the flaps. We had lots of runway, so I didn't say anything. I latched the door. Edgar called the tower.

"Alpha Nan Dog, takeoff."

"Cleared for takeoff, Alpha November Delta, wind two four zero at twelve."

Edgar zipped onto the runway and hauled the control wheel into his chest. He hunched forward like a jockey riding a horse and applied full power and right rudder. The Cherokee's nose came up almost immediately in response to the stabilator. We accelerated down the runway tail low like a Cub on a short field takeoff. The airplane lifted off in ground effect. Edgar lowered the nose and held it there while we accelerated to 85 mph. Then he set up a climb.

I asked him to head for the practice area ten miles southeast of the airport and climb to 3,500 feet. He flew the airplane well. He coordinated the rudder and ailerons better than most Cherokee pilots. When he levelled off, he set the throttle to 2100 rpm and cruised along nose high.

"Why so low a power setting?" I asked.

He looked at me with a frown and spoke with the sharpness of the impatient old person that he was.

"Are you in a hurry?" he asked.

"No."

"Are you paying for the gas?"

"No."

"Is there anything wrong with this cruise setting?"

"You'll need more power for turns."

"When we turn, I'll add it," he said sharply.

"Okay, show me a 90 degree turn to the left just for practice."

Edgar nodded, added full power, glanced left and rolled the Cherokee into a 90-degree bank. He hauled back on the control wheel, pressing us into our seats.

I realized right away that he thought I had meant 90-degree bank when I had asked for a turn. I didn't say anything. I wondered how long he could hold the turn before the stubby-winged Piper fell out of the sky.

The answer was 180 degrees. Edgar hung onto our altitude at the expense of a rapidly decaying airspeed. After half a circle, I thought the Cherokee would flick into a spin to the right but Edgar rolled out of the turn before it did.

"Want one to the right?" he asked smartly. He left full power on. The airplane regained its lost speed.

"Sure," I answered.

Edgar looked right, flipped the Cherokee on its right side and hauled it around. He rolled out 180 degrees later.

Not bad for an old guy, I thought to myself.

"What's next?" he barked.

I had forgotten that this was a proficiency check on a pension. He was making sure that I didn't waste any time.

"Do a stall," I replied.

Edgar cut the power and hauled the nose up high. The stall horn sounded, the airplane shuddered and the nose dropped. Edgar shoved the throttle in and recovered on the edge of a secondary stall. He immediately gave me a "what's next" look.

"You should check for traffic below before practising stalls," I said.

"We didn't lose any altitude," he quickly replied.

He was right.

"Do the same thing with power on in the stall," I said.

Edgar obliged. When the Cherokee started to buffet with its nose pointed skyward, I pushed my right rudder pedal. The wing dropped and the airplane snapped into one almighty spin. Edgar held it in. The horizon rotated in the windshield. I looked at him. He looked at me.

"You put it in sonny," he yelled. "Let me know when you want out."
We were into our third rotation.

"Recover," I said loudly.

Edgar stuffed the nose down and stomped on left rudder. He cut the power and pulled out of the dive.

"Leave the power off," I said. "Let's practise a simulated forced approach. Pick a field and we'll fly down to 500 feet."

Without answering he quickly found a field and set up an old style spiral approach around the chosen landing spot.

"Do you have an emergency drill for a forced approach?" I asked.

"We're doing it," he replied.

"How about getting the engine restarted or radioing a 'Mayday'?"

"Well, the only problem with the engine is the throttle is at idle so I don't want to be alerting nobody for that," he said flatly.

I didn't argue.

At one thousand feet, Edgar applied right rudder to create a slipping turn to a base leg to the field. It was obvious to both of us that we would make the landing.

"Overshoot," I said, "and head back to the airport for circuits."

When we were established in the airport circuit pattern, I asked Edgar to set up for the type of landing that he would have used during an actual forced approach. I took over the radio work and gave the instructor code for a practice overshoot. On the final leg of the approach, Edgar slowed the Cherokee down to 65 mph and plowed toward the runway with the nose high and power on. He had not extended the flaps so he was flying the laminar flow wing well below the power curve. It was going to be a difficult transition to an overshoot.

On short final, the controller called, "Alpha November Delta, pull up and go around, pull up and go around!"

Edgar continued the approach. He looked at the runway. He looked up and down the cross runways. There was no other traffic. He cut the power. The Cherokee dropped on the numbers.

"You were supposed to overshoot," I declared.

"There was no reason to overshoot," he answered impatiently.

"For practice."

"He didn't say that."

"He shouldn't have too."

"Are we done?"

"No. One more circuit for a crosswind landing on Runway 28."

"Nice overshoot, Alpha November Delta," the controller said. "What do you want to do now?"

Edgar applied full power.

"I see you're taking off," the controller said calmly. "Advise your intentions."

"Alpha November Delta requests a circuit on Runway 28 for a full stop," I said.

"Approved November Delta. You're cleared to land Runway 28, wind 240 at 10."

"November Delta."

Edgar kept the circuit in tight. On the final leg for Runway 28, he set up a crab to the left rather than a sideslip to compensate for the crosswind. He flew this into the flareout, touched down on the left tire and then pushed right rudder. This yawed the nose and pointed it straight down the runway. The speed dropped and the right wheel came down against the left aileron he was holding. Then the nose wheel dropped on the runway.

It was the old style "crab/kick" crosswind landing.

Edgar's flying was ropy and out-of-date but he made it work. I decided that trying to improve his technique would be a self-inflicted negative experience.

"Nicely done," I said to Edgar. "That's it."

"Cleared to the ramp, November Delta," the controller said.

"November Delta."

I signed him off for another year.

Chapter Ten

Top guns

The Snowbirds came to town. The Canadian Forces Air Demonstration Team flew an air show at the Derry Airport on a sunny Saturday in June. I first heard they were coming from Eric.

"Make sure you leave the third Friday in June open for Angel's party."

"Angel's party? Eric, the two words don't belong in the same sentence."

Angel was a spectacularly homely and overweight spinster who ran the flying school with a tenacious efficiency. Except for church on Sundays, squatting on a stool behind the flight desk and living with her parents on the farm next to the airport seemed to be her whole life. Angel was not the party type.

"Yah. She has a barbecue when the Snowbirds come to town. It's a tradition."

"So the Snowbirds are coming and they stay for a barbecue at Angel's? Eric, I think you've been in the sun too long."

"Trust me. They arrive on the day before their show, fly a practice with the media and then go to Angel's barbecue at the farm. All the Derry Air staff are invited. Keep it open."

"Okay, I will."

Shortly after that, posters went up announcing the Snowbirds' air show. At our next staff meeting, Derry Air owner Irving Mingy explained that the regular flying would be suspended that day and the instructors would split their time between talking to the public about lessons and doing sightseeing flights. At the end of the meeting, Angel passed around invitations to the Friday barbecue. The bottom of the notice said the cost was five dollars per person.

"When did we start charging for staff parties?" I asked Eric afterward.

He smiled knowingly. "This is much more than a staff party. The proceeds go to church work. It's worth it."

"Okay."

I still planned to go mainly because I wanted to find out why the Snowbirds, the pilot mega-jocks, would adjust their schedule to attend a party thrown by an ugly, middle-aged, church-going wallflower.

I was working at the airport on Friday when the team arrived. The back row of the Derry Air ramp had been cleared of airplanes. Linecrew Huey, Duey and Louey had spent the morning sweeping the area. The team coordinator and the announcer landed first in the two advance airplanes. They taxied to the designated parking area and shut down. Angel had departed her stool and was standing on the ramp with the Derry mayor, the airport manager and several local dignitaries. I stood watching by the flying school front door with a few customers and staff. Spectators from the flying school in the next hangar were nearby.

The two pilots climbed out of their brightly-painted jets and walked straight to Angel. They each gave her a big hug. It was the first time I had seen her smile. She handed them each an invitation to her barbecue. Then they shook hands with the other members of the welcoming party. While they were doing that, the nine-airplane Snowbird team flew overhead. They broke formation and lined up nose to tail for a landing. The red and white jets touched down one after the other in quick succession and gathered at the end of the runway before taxiing in as a group.

Angel walked over to the front of their parking area as they filed onto the ramp. She stood there with her flowered tent dress blowing in the breeze while the line of airplanes turned to face her in perfect unison. They flashed their landing lights and shut down. Still in unison, the canopies opened upwards, the pilots and crew chiefs travelling with them removed their helmets, climbed out and stood smartly at attention beside their airplanes. They looked sharp in their fitted red flight suits and angled caps. Angel walked to Snowbird Number One, gave the pilot and his technician a big hug and a party invitation. She repeated this along the entire nine-plane line. Each crew waited for her before moving forward to greet the other dignitaries.

When all the hand shaking was done, the team went back to their airplanes to dig out their gear. A bus pulled onto the ramp to take them to their hotel downtown.

At Eric's suggestion, I arranged for my wife Susan to meet me at the flying school at the end of the day. "Oh boy," she said sarcastically, "a party full of pilots."

"We don't have to stay long," I replied.

Eric had warned me that there was no parking at the farm so Susan and

I walked over from Derry Air. The county road leading to the farm was blocked solid with cars and pedestrians. We walked up the laneway as part of a steady stream of people going to the party. When we rounded the corner of the farmhouse, we couldn't believe our eyes. The three-acre back yard was filled with people. Tables were set up near the back of the house and piled high with food.

Two ladies at a card table took our five dollars and stamped the back of our hands. "Help yourself to punch over there," one of them said, "and don't go hungry."

Except for a couple of Derry Air staff, Susan and I did not know anyone in the crowd. "These people are all single," Susan said as we lined up for some punch.

"How do you know?" I asked.

"Look around. The women are standing in groups separate from the men. Most of them are young or they have that 'never married' look."

I found out later that Angel's annual Snowbird party had grown from the first year when she had announced to the Church Women's League that the air show pilots would be at her house. After that, word got out to the single male population in Derry that all the single females in town would be at the party.

"Most of the women are dressed in red and white," Susan observed, "and the men are wearing aviator sunglasses."

She was right. Angel's back yard was filling up with female Snowbird groupies and male would-be top gun pilots.

While we were standing and eating, the Snowbirds flew overhead. Everyone watched while they centred their practice show on the back yard of Angels parents' house.

When they were done, I asked Susan if she was ready to go home. "No, I want to meet the Snowbirds," she said with a smile.

"It could be an hour before they secure their airplanes and get over here," I said.

"That's okay," she replied looking at a group of men wearing tight jeans, "there's lots to see while we're waiting."

Chapter Eleven

Pilot

Darcy Philips had a dog. She was a pert little brown and white Border Collie that came to Derry Air with the chief mechanic every day. "Pilot" helped out in the shop as a parts runner. When a mechanic working on an airplane needed something, he wrote it on a piece of paper and whistled for Pilot. The dog would jump up from her mat in Darcy's office and streak to the workstation. She'd take the note in her mouth and run to the parts department. Brenda, the Derry Air parts girl, would drop the parts into a "doggy bag" and hold it for Pilot. The little dog would trot back to the mechanic with the bag in her mouth. She'd drop the delivery at the mechanic's feet, sit down and bark once. The mechanic who reached for the parts bag before tossing a treat would get more barks.

The system worked well and Pilot loved doing it. The Derry Air maintenance hangar was usually a tangle of airplanes. Pilot could dart under the wings and make it to the back in less time than one of the lumbering maintenance staff. Darcy taught her to roll the small aircraft tires with her nose. Brenda placed large items in boxes. It was not unusual to see her dragging a box of hoses or weatherstripping by its flap, her little legs digging constantly. If she was stopped by an air hose, she'd bark for help.

"Why did you name her 'Pilot'?" I asked the sarcastic mechanic one day.

"Because she's stupid," he replied with a smirk.

"That's not true," I said. "She's the smartest dog I've ever seen."

"Oh yah? Watch this." Darcy whistled. Pilot was at his feet in a flash, her tail wagging in anticipation of pleasing somebody. "Get me a half-inch, open-end wrench," Darcy said to her. He waved toward his toolbox. The little collie bounded to the big red cabinet and hopped up to the shelf on the side. She picked up a wooden-handled screwdriver from the top compartment with her teeth, jumped down and ran over to Darcy. She sat

75

up with the tool in her mouth.

Judging from the teeth marks in the handle, they had done this routine many times. Darcy reached down and took the screwdriver. He held it up for me. "See? She's dumb as a pilot. She can't tell the difference between a wrench and a screwdriver."

Chapter Twelve

"Don't touch anything"

One evening Derry Air manager Irving Mingy spoke to me when I was finishing with my last student. An urgent call had come in for a flight to deliver three passengers to Baie Comeau, Quebec on the north shore of the St. Lawrence River.

"Fly a charter to Baie Comeau with Perry in the Navajo," Mingy said. He made it a statement, not a request.

It was the end of a long day. I had just finished night circuits with the student. I was tired and looking forward to going home but suddenly all that didn't matter. The chance to fly in the large twin-engine Piper revived me. It didn't matter that I had no clue where Baie Comeau was. It didn't matter that I had a total of five minutes in the Navajo.

"Yes sir," I replied.

It mattered to Perry Butcher, Derry Air's chief charter pilot. Normally his copilots were qualified on the Navajo. They did all the planning, flying and radio work. Perry went along for the ride and collected his pay. Having me assigned to the flight meant that he was sentenced to work all night. He would have to stay awake, fly and baby-sit a neophyte copilot.

When Mingy told me to do the trip, Perry was on the phone filing a flight plan. The three passengers were waiting by the front door with their overnight bags. I ducked into my briefing cubicle and grabbed my shiny new kneeboard with its inlaid stopwatch and reading light from my flight bag. I fed the vending machine all of my change and came away with two chocolate bars.

Perry finished on the phone, picked up the company flight bag and headed for the door. "All set," he said to the passengers. He ignored me. They nodded and followed him outside. I brought up the rear.

Perry was short, stocky and middle-aged. He marched out to the Navajo under the ramp lights. One beefy arm carried the heavy flight bag and the other one swung around his overloaded mid-section. I knew little about him except that he was a down-on-his-luck kind of guy. In better days he had been a trim fighter pilot in the air force and married with children. Now he was fat, double-divorced and broke. When Perry split with his first wife, a judge awarded her the house, the kids and half of Perry's money. When he split with his second wife, a judge gave her the car and the other half of the money. Now he lived in an old trailer in the Derry Air parking lot. He flew charters for cash. The arrangement suited Mingy. With no car and no money, Perry was always there. When there was a call for a flight, the Derry Air owner just had to bang on the trailer.

Perry dropped the bag on the ramp and opened the airstair door on the left side of the cabin. He told the passengers to sit anywhere. He turned to start a walkaround inspection of the airplane.

"What would you like me to do?" I asked politely.

He hesitated for a second. He was having trouble remembering that he had a copilot and that I was it.

"Get in, sit down and don't touch anything," he growled.

He walked around the wing with a flashlight in hand. I climbed on board, squeezed between the passengers who were settling into the seats on each side of the cabin and slid into the copilot seat. I could see that Perry had made it around to the right engine already and was checking the oil. I fished out my seat belt, strapped on my kneeboard and looked at the instrument panel. There were gauges galore. I had made it to the big time. It was going to be hard to go back to a Cherokee after this flight.

I soon heard Perry closing the cabin door and pushing his way to the front. He squeezed into the left seat with a few grunts but no conversation. As he plopped onto the cushion, he started to snap switches on. The cockpit came alive with instrument noises and lights. Perry dug out his seat belt with one hand and started the left engine with the other. As the engine settled down to idle, he fired up the right side. Then he flipped on the avionics master switch and twirled the frequency selector of the number one communication radio.

"Anything I can do to help?" I asked hopefully. I thought at least I could handle the communications.

"No. Just sit there and don't touch anything," Perry said. He reached for the headset behind him.

"How about I go to the back and retrieve the flight bag off the ramp?" I asked.

Perry looked down between our seats to where the flight bag should have been. Then he looked at me. I didn't move. He was going to have to ask.

"Okay," he said and then he pulled the mixture to kill the left engine.

I undid my belt, twisted out of the seat and walked to the back in a

crouch. The passengers were already trying to catch some sleep. I flopped the door down, grabbed the bag, closed the door and returned to the cockpit. Perry restarted the left engine while I did my seat belt up and donned the headset.

"Dig me out the eastbound charts, will ya?" Perry asked. There was no "please" or "thank you" but I felt like I was making progress.

The big pilot called Derry Ground Control, taxied out, did a quick runup check, copied instrument flight clearance and took off. On the climb, he held his hand out for the charts. I gave him the first map. He snapped

79

the autopilot on and set up the navigation radios. We climbed to 11,000 feet and levelled off.

"Switch to Centre frequency 134.25," the controller said.

"One three four point two five," Perry replied. He spun the selector and punched the transmit button. "Toronto Centre, Derry One is with you at eleven thousand."

There was no reply.

I spoke up. "He said 'one three four point two five'," I said, pointing to the radio.

Perry had selected the wrong frequency. He flicked the dial and repeated the call.

"Radar contact," the controller replied.

There wasn't much other traffic on the frequency. Perry reached over to my side of the instrument panel and punched in the cigarette lighter. He pulled out a pack of Players Straight Cut and stuck one in his mouth. When the lighter popped, he pulled it out and lit his weed.

We passed by Oshawa, Stirling and Kingston, Ontario. Perry set up the navigation and communication frequencies while the autopilot flew the airplane. I thought of asking him if I could hand-fly since he wasn't but I kept quiet. The routine with the cigarettes and the lighter was repeated every 20 minutes. I was thoroughly bored and was getting sleepy. Toronto switched us to Boston Center as we crossed over the St. Lawrence River. Perry changed the frequency. It had been fifteen minutes since the last cigarette. For something to do, I punched in the lighter. Perry automatically pulled out a cigarette. The Navajo droned on into the night. The only other thing I could find to do was hand him a new chart as we flew off the old one. To stay awake, I repeated the lighter routine, a minute shorter each time. When we passed Sherbrooke, I had Perry down to a cigarette every five minutes.

It was after midnight. There was no other traffic on the radio. I was getting very sleepy. I offered Perry a chocolate bar. He accepted. I ate the other one. It revived me briefly.

"Want me to work the radios for you?" I asked hopefully.

"No thanks," was the short reply.

"If you give me the map back, I could set up the nav frequencies for you as we went along," I suggested.

"No, it's all right."

I gave up and went back to punching the lighter, increasing the intervals this time.

"It's foggy in Baie Comeau," Perry suddenly said. "When we get there, you can call the runway lights for me on the approach."

He was throwing me a crumb at last.

"Sure," I replied. "I'd be glad to." I punched the lighter. He pulled out

a cigarette.

The Navajo continued to bore holes into the night. I thought about being ready for the lights at Baie Comeau. The last thing I remember was pushing the lighter near Quebec City. I had been fighting to stay awake for some time. The cigarette intervals were up to 23 minutes. I fell asleep. My head rolled on my chest while the shoulder harness held me in the upright position. Perry let me snore all the way to Baie Comeau. He set up a descent and shot an ILS approach to Runway 10. It was foggy as forecasted.

Just before reaching the minimum approach height, Perry saw the runway lights. He cut the power on the two engines. The sudden change in sound woke me up. My eyes popped open. The first thing I saw were twin rows of lights down each side of the runway in the swirling fog. Perry flared the airplane for the touchdown.

"Lights! Lights! Lights!" I shouted at the top of my lungs.

The screaming copilot routine caused Perry to balloon the landing. The Navajo kangarooed down the runway. He managed to regain control before doing any damage.

Perry taxied the airplane to the ramp and shut down. He got out of his seat and opened the door for the passengers without saying anything to me. I could feel my face was red. I sat in the cockpit while he arranged for fuel. The realization that we were about to fly all the way back to Derry forced me out of my seat to go to the airport washroom. I went back outside and stood by the Navajo door in the cool, damp air until Perry was ready to go again.

"Get in," he barked. "Don't touch anything and don't say anything."

Chapter Thirteen

Doomer

D^{*ear Sir;*}

It has been brought to the attention of this department that your neurological medical condition is not up to the standards of your aircrew certificate. Please submit to a psychiatric examination and have a report submitted within 60 days. The status of your fitness to hold an aircrew certificate will then be reviewed. If a report is not submitted in time, the privileges of your certificate will be suspended.
Sincerely,
Cameron I. Kazie MD
Director Regional Aviation Medicine

The letter, typed on official government letterhead, had been sent to Eric. He handed it around during a coffee break.

"It came from the aviation medicine office but I smell Inspector Kennedy trying to get even," Eric said. He didn't sound very worried about the prospect of losing his pilot licence.

"Is this a result of your ballistic response to Kennedy during his base inspection?" Henry asked.

"Sure," the CFI said. "Then he had to fly with our friend here in a snow storm after cancelling a good weather flight test. The score is Derry Air 2, Kennedy 1."

"I'll sign your medical report," I offered. "I can certify that you're crazy."

"Thanks for nothing," he replied. "If I lose my licence, one of you guys will have to do my job."

"Okay, I take that back," I said. "So what are you going to do?"

"Call in the secret weapon," Eric said. Henry smiled knowingly.

"You lost me on that one," I said.

"Doctor Roy," Henry offered.

"Our Doctor Roy who does the pilot medicals?"

"The same," Eric replied. "Whenever the government rides its high horse with us, we get Roy to write the response."

Dr. Lee Roy was the local designated aviation medical examiner. The ex-air force flight surgeon was an older man but sharp as a tack and fitter than most pilots. He was full of bustle but he also had a spirited sense of humour. I had met him at my last medical. He ordered me to lose five kilos or to grow taller to fit my weight. Dr. Roy was a frequent visitor to Derry Air. His office was near the airport and he kept an airplane in our hangar.

After our coffee break, Eric called the doctor's office and left a message with the nurse asking Roy to drop by.

The doctor came into the Derry Air lounge on Wednesday afternoon.

Eric showed him the letter.

He smiled. "What did you do to bring this on?" he asked, handing the letter back.

"I got short with one of the inspectors during a base inspection last month," Eric admitted.

"Kennedy?" Dr. Roy asked.

"Yah, how did you know?"

"The only thing reliable about the Department of Transport in this region is Kennedy. You can always count on that miserable piece of humanity to give you a hard time. I knew him in the air force. His nickname was 'Doomer'."

"'Doomer', it fits. So how do we handle this?" Eric asked. "I don't want to lose my licence. Not yet, anyway."

"The best defence is offence. I'll write a letter for you to send back. You'll never hear from them again."

"Thanks, Doc."

"You're welcome. Now you can help me. I want to go flying and Huey, Duey and Louey are hiding again. Help me get my airplane out from the back of the hangar."

"Right away!" Eric replied.

Dr. Roy dropped a letter off by the end of the week. Eric showed it to me before he sent it.

Department of Transport
Director Regional Aviation Medicine
Dear Sir;
I have examined Eric Daedalus as requested. I found no psychosis, neurosis or behavior disorder. His excellent physical and mental condition exceeds the department's standards for his level of aircrew certificate.

These findings bring into question the mental state of the person who reported otherwise. I suggest that the individual is seriously out of line and possibly suffering from a sub-standard mental capacity of their own. Only someone mentally deficient would undertake an unqualified, non-clinical, potentially career-ending assessment of Mr. Daedalus.

It bothers me to discover that your department retains such a loose cannon as a staff member. This raises serious questions about the department's hiring practices and employee monitoring.

If Mr. Daedalus ever develops a neurosis, it could be easily argued that it was brought on by dealing with overzealous and incompetent department inspection staff. This is a liability that the Minister of Transport may not want to bear.

In addition, your letter to Mr. Daedalus indirectly questions the integrity of your Designated Aviation Medical Examiners program. Mr. Daedalus attended a routine pilot examination recently. The physician found him physically and mentally qualified to exceed the standards of his medical category at that time. Your subsequent request for further examination, although within your power, questions the quality of work performed by the attending examiner. If you intend to question other findings of this doctor based on the heresy of unqualified, mentally deficient staff members I would like to know because I am that examiner. If Mr. Daedalus and I don't hear from you in 30 days, I will assume that my standards of examination are once again acceptable and I will know that I'm not wasting my time any more and neither are you.

Sincerely,
Dr. Lee Roy

"This is beautiful," I said. "It's a work of art."

"I know," Eric replied. "I'm going to frame it and send a copy to Dr. Kazie."

He did.

The next day, Larry Buttons returned from holidays.

"What did you think of the joke letter I sent you?" he asked Eric.

"What 'joke' letter?"

"The April Fool's medical letter."

Chapter Fourteen

Jet pilot

It was a soggy day at Derry. A massive warm front blanketed the area with low cloud and drizzle. The forecast called for solid stratus up to 10,000 feet.

It would have been a great day for instrument flying but I didn't have an IFR student. I had Melville Passmore, Derry Air's marathon student. Melville's biggest problem was that farm smarts didn't count for much when it came to obtaining a pilot licence. The government had made it an academic achievement and Melville had not gone very far in school.

The little farmer and I never cancelled a lesson if the weather was bad. We did ground briefings which is what we were doing around noon when Skid Sicamore burst into the flight lounge.

Skid was the local aircraft broker with a reputation that matched his first name. The slimy salesman glided straight to the front counter. His rumpled trench coat flapped with each hurried step. Angel was squatting on her stool behind the flight desk doing paperwork.

"Gimme an airplane and two pilots right away," Sicamore demanded.

From across the room, I was half listening to him and half to Melville. We were the only ones in the office. The rest of the staff had taken advantage of weather cancellations and driven to town for lunch.

Melville was reviewing the documents required on board an airplane. After two years of lessons, we were finally getting ready for his flight test.

"I got an instructor doing a ground briefing," Angel replied to the impatient broker. "The rest are down the road at lunch."

Sicamore looked my way. "Hey you two," he called over. "How about an airplane ride?"

Melville was slowly trying to explain the difference between air time and flight time entries in the Aircraft Journey Logbook. I interrupted him.

"What's up, Skid?" I called back.

"I got a Lear Jet to pick up from London," he said. "I need a ride there and another pilot to fly back with me."

The words "Lear Jet" galvanized me. The chance to ride in one of those hot corporate aircraft was not something I would pass up. Sicamore was talking possible front-seat turbine time.

I ignored Melville, stood up and headed across the room.

"There is nobody at Derry Air qualified on anything like a Lear Jet, Skid," I said.

He waved his arm in an erasing motion. "They don't have to be," he said impatiently. "I just want a face in the right seat window to keep the government happy. If you fly me to London, all I need is another body to ride back with me." He looked nervously at his watch. "I've got to be back here by two o'clock."

My mind was racing. Maybe I couldn't bag Lear time out of this but at least I could clock an hour or so of revenue instrument flying.

I looked at Melville. He was hunched over the logbook with his tongue hanging out. He looked like he was wishing for more information to jump off the page and into his head.

"I'd be happy to fly you to London, Skid. Captain Passmore over there can ride back with you in the jet."

"Okay, sport, let's go."

"On one condition," I added.

"What's that?" he frowned.

"We take the Twin Comanche. It's faster."

It was also a lot more useful in my logbook.

"Is it out and ready to go?"

I could see Derry Air's twin engine trainer sitting on the ramp.

"Yes, sir, it is."

"Good stuff," Sicamore said. He turned to Angel. She was holding out the logbook. He grabbed it.

"I'll file a flight plan," I said. "You might as well file yours now too."

"Good thinking," Sicamore said. He picked up the telephone and punched the speed dial to flight service.

"Three IFR flight plans," he barked. "Two for Derry Air's Twin Comanche: Derry direct London and back, minimum altitudes, 30 minutes each way, leaving now, coming right back, three and one on board. Everything else is on file here at Derry Air. The third plan is for a Lear 24 slash everything, London to Derry at 15,000, 500 mph, two on board, minimum fuel, pilot Sicamore. If you need anything else, catch it in the air." He hung up without waiting for a reply.

"All set!" he said to me. It wasn't a question. He was already headed for the door.

I hotfooted over to the briefing cubicle and grabbed my flight bag.

"Melville, leave that for now. We're going for an airplane ride. We'll be back before the end of your lesson."

Melville never needed a second invitation to fly.

"Okay."

I hustled him across the office and out the door. We headed toward the Twin Comanche on the other side of the ramp. Its left engine started. The airplane immediately moved forward. Melville and I stepped aside as Sicamore swung the low-wing Piper around us.

"You climb in first and get in the back," I yelled to Melville.

I followed him onto the right wing. As I dropped into the right seat, Sicamore started the right engine.

"I already called ground," he said. "They don't have our clearance yet so we're going to taxi to Runway 24 while we're waiting."

The beginning of Runway 24 was further away but it would launch us toward London.

This was obviously going to be a typical Skid flight: no preparation, no charts, no walkaround and no consideration for the system and the others in it. Sicamore was demonstrating everything about pilots that air traffic controllers loved to hate.

I turned around. Melville was fumbling to fasten his belt in the right rear seat. I reached over with my flight bag and dropped it beside him. The farm boy's eyes were wide. Everything that Melville was witnessing went against his two years of flight training.

Sicamore blasted down the taxiway. The radio speaker crackled to life. "IFR clearance, Alpha India Romeo."

The microphone was in Sicamore's lap. He picked it up. "Go ahead," he replied.

"ATC clears Delta Alpha India Romeo to the London Airport, Derry direct, maintain four thousand, depart Runway 24, right turn on course, squawk 5515, contact Toronto Centre 133.3."

Sicamore read the clearance back without writing it down.

"Readback correct, India Romeo, call the tow..."

Sicamore cut off the controller by changing the frequency. "We're ready to go," he radioed to the tower controller. He timed our taxi speed to hit the runway without stopping.

"Cleared for takeoff, Alpha India Romeo, wind zero nine zero at five to ten."

Sicamore zoomed onto the runway without replying and hit full power. The Twin Comanche accelerated smartly. We were barely at flying speed when the salesman hauled the control wheel back. He forced the airplane into the air and snapped the landing gear lever up.

I set the transponder code and turned it on and then tuned in the London VOR. Sicamore started a right turn on course at 300 feet. We were in the clag at 500.

"Contact Toronto Centre, Alpha India Romeo."

Sicamore flew direct to London using full throttle all the way. Melville sat wide-eyed but quiet in the back.

"Mr. Sicamore wants you to ride with him from London to Derry in a Lear Jet," I said over the engine roar. "I didn't think you'd mind some right seat time in a jet."

The little farmer's eyes grew wider. He was too shy to say anything out loud. He pointed at himself and then thrust his hand through the air while blowing through his lips. He was miming, "Me? In a jet?"

"Yes," I replied.

The chubby face lit up.

When I had a few minutes, I thought about the return trip. I could either fly back at 40 per cent power and log as much twin-engine time as possible or see if I could beat Sicamore. I decided the latter would be more fun. I'd race Sicamore back to Derry. The 200-mph Twin Comanche versus a 500-mph Lear Jet.

Approaching London, Sicamore requested and received radar vectors for a straight-in instrument approach to Runway 33. He kept the power on and accelerated during the descent. Sicamore locked on the localizer just before we crossed the beacon on a four-mile final. He chopped the power. The short exhaust pipes on the twin Lycomings snapped, crackled and popped. Then he stabbed the landing gear lever down.

We broke out of the cloud at 400 feet. Sicamore shoved the nose down and dropped below the glide path. He aimed to land short. He drove the airplane onto the runway numbers at speed, locked the brakes on the wet surface and skidded into the first exit. We were pointed toward the terminal building. He continued on to the ramp without calling the ground controller and headed for a Lear Jet. He swung the Twin Comanche around and stopped.

"Okay, let's go," he barked.

I was between him and the door. Before getting out, I reached over to the pilot side and set the parking brake and then shut down the right engine. "I'll race you back," I said.

"Sure, sure," Sicamore said quickly. "But first you have to let us out."

"Ten bucks says I get back first."

Now he was paying attention. He looked at me. His face broke into a thin smile. "You're on, hotshot."

I climbed onto the right wing and held the door open while Skid and Melville squeezed out. I jumped back in, latched the door and slid over to the left seat. As I restarted the right engine, I could see the aircraft salesman opening the two-piece door on the Lear.

I strapped on my clipboard and radioed London Clearance Delivery requesting an IFR Clearance to Derry.

"ATC clears Delta Alpha India Romeo to the Derry Airport, London direct, maintain five thousand, off Runway Three Three, right turn on course, squawk 5523, Toronto Centre 135.3."

A puff of smoke from the back of the Lear indicated that Sicamore was already starting his engines.

I read the clearance back.

"Clearance correct, India Romeo," the controller said. "Call ground. He has a few choice words for you about your arrival."

"Different pilot," I replied.

As I reached for the radio selector, Sicamore broke in on the frequency requesting his clearance. The Lear Jet was already moving forward. Sicamore was trying to go around me. I quickly released the brakes and squirted in front of him.

"London Ground," I radioed, "Alpha India Romeo, taxi on an IFR flight to Derry."

"You guys might consider calling first and then taxiing," the controller said sarcastically. "Runway 33, Alpha India Romeo. Taxi via Golf. Check the Lear Jet behind you is not on the frequency."

"Alpha India Romeo."

At the time London did not have a terminal control or radar. The key to my beating Sicamore was staying ahead of him and blocking his progress.

Sicamore called ground control and asked for taxi instructions for an intersection departure on Runway 33 from taxiway Hotel. This was granted but I immediately switched to the tower frequency and said I was ready to go even though I had not reached the runway. The controller bought it.

"Position and hold for radar release Alpha India Romeo."

Sicamore called ready for takeoff while approaching from the next intersection down the runway. He was told to hold short.

As soon as I had taxied onto the runway, I received a take-off clearance. "Toronto Centre airborne," the controller added.

I applied full power. The lightly loaded twin accelerated smartly. As I passed the Lear Jet, I could see a familiar round face in the right side. It looked like Melville was fumbling for his seat belt.

I pulled back on the control wheel. The Comanche jumped into the air and zoomed into the cloud. As soon as the ground disappeared, I turned right on course but I didn't call Toronto Centre. Until I was in communication with the area controller, Sicamore would not be allowed to take off.

One minute later, London tower called and asked if I was still on the frequency. I ignored him. I switched to Toronto Centre, waited a few more seconds and then called. I spoke slowly.

"Toronto Centre, this is Twin Comanche Charlie Delta Alpha India

91

Romeo, off London Runway 33 in a right turn." I purposely omitted my altitude which was what the controller needed to release the Lear Jet.

"Say your altitude India Romeo."

"India Romeo is through 2,000 feet for 5,000."

"Call level."

"India Romeo."

The controller would then call London Tower via landline and release the Lear Jet for takeoff. I motored on up to 5,000 feet. When I levelled off, I left the throttles wide open. The constant speed propellers automatically cycled to a coarser pitch. The twin accelerated. It was the first time I had seen over 200 mph on the airspeed indicator.

"Alpha India Romeo level five thousand."

"Radar contact."

Sicamore's voice came on the frequency. "Toronto, Lear Juliet Excho Tango off London out of two thousand for fifteen thousand looking for the right turn."

"Juliet Echo Tango, roger. Call out of five thousand."

"Out of five thousand," Sicamore said immediately.

I imagined that Sicamore had started the right turn anyway while he was below Toronto's radar coverage.

"Right turn on course, Echo Tango."

Sicamore didn't reply.

"Echo Tango," the controller said, "I'm not getting your transponder. Confirm squawking code 5530?"

"We are now."

"Radar contact."

Derry was 50 nautical miles east of London; 20 minutes for me and eight minutes for Sicamore and Melville in the Lear Jet. When I was approaching half way, I was switched to the next IFR sector controller. It was early for an approach, but I called for one anyway.

"Toronto Centre, Alpha India Romeo is looking for vectors for the straight in Runway 06 at Derry."

"Check that, India Romeo. Turn right 10 degrees for radar vectors to Derry. Expect the straight in Runway 06."

"Heading one zero zero radar vectors Derry," I said. "India Romeo."

I turned five degrees. I wanted to keep it in tight. The Automatic Direction Finder showed the Derry non-directional beacon on the nose.

Sicamore checked in on the frequency.

"Juliet Echo Tango," the controller replied. "Confirm you're level fifteen thousand."

"Level fifteen," Sicamore said impatiently. "We'll take an approach."

This was the point where the race could go either way. The Derry Airport didn't have radar. Only one aircraft would be allowed on the approach at a time.

"Toronto, Alpha India Romeo will take a descent anytime."

The controller gave it to me.

"Alpha India Romeo turn further right to one one zero degrees, you're cleared to the Derry Airport for the straight in ILS Runway 06. Descend pilot discretion."

I read the clearance back and eased the nose down. I only turned five degrees. The speed went to 220 mph.

"Juliet Echo Tango, you might as well slow down. You'll be number two on the approach to Derry behind a Twin Comanche."

"Echo Tango."

"Alpha India Romeo, you're looking tight to the marker. You can turn another ten degrees right or intercept the localizer one mile back."

"We'll keep it in tight."

"Okay, over to tower now, one twenty-five zero."

The race was over. The only way I could lose was to miss the approach. I throttled back and switched frequencies. Derry Tower gave me the latest weather. The ceiling was 500 feet. I had it made.

I intercepted the localizer and the glideslope, dropped the landing gear and crossed the beacon final almost at the same time. I was cleared to land Runway 06.

The Twin Comanche popped out of the cloud. I was lined up with the runway. I cut the power, flared out and touched down. I rolled out to the next intersection, turned off and called ground control. On the long taxi around to the ramp, I gloated over beating Sicamore at his own game. I imagined the Lear Jet on the approach now. Melville was probably still trying to do up his seat belt.

Out of the corner of my eye I saw movement in the distance through the mist. I turned. It was the Lear Jet. Sicamore had landed on Runway 24 which ended next to the Derry Air ramp. He must have asked for radar vectors around to the opposite end of the runway that I was using after I had switched frequencies. The downwind approach and landing had given him a straight shot to the ramp.

I speeded up my taxiing but I was too late. The Lear Jet was already parked when I pulled onto the ramp. Melville was standing next to it sporting a huge grin. He thrust both arms triumphantly in the air. They had won.

Chapter Fifteen

Edgar the astronaut

Edgar Edgar, Derry Air's 87 year old rental pilot was returning from another of his monthly flights when Eric and I were in the lounge.

"Hi Edgar," I said casually. "Did you have a good flight?"

"Eh?"

"Did you have a good flight?" I boomed.

"Fair to middling," he said. Then he pulled a small envelope from his coat pocket. "I brought pictures from last month to show you."

The envelope didn't look very thick so Eric and I pretended to be interested. Edgar pulled out two photos. They were aerial shots taken straight down from what appeared to be a high altitude. Closer inspection revealed that Niagara Falls was in the middle of the photos. The Horseshoe Falls was the size of a baby fingernail and the city surrounding it was a tiny mosaic of streets and railroad tracks. The scene was dotted with little puffs of cumulus clouds floating far below the level of the photographer.

"Ah... did you take these Edgar?" Eric asked.

"Eh?"

"Did you take these pictures?!"

"Yah," he answered loudly. He pointed at the shot Eric was holding. "It's Niagara Falls. You can see it in the middle."

Eric and I looked at each other. There was no wing in the pictures. Edgar must have been circling in a very steep turn at high altitude steering with his knees and shooting out the side window.

"How high were you flying for these shots Edgar?"

"Oh, around eighteen thousand. The Cherokee won't go much higher. Not and turn. The Cub was a better airplane for altitude."

"You can't fly at 18,000 feet, Edgar," Eric said.

"Sure I can. I do it all the time. You can see a long way from up there."

"I mean, it's against the air regulations to fly above 12,500 feet with-

out an instrument rating, an ATC clearance and supplemental oxygen."

Edgar frowned. "When did they start that nonsense?"

"I think it's been a while, Edgar. Don't you find it hard to breathe at 18,000 feet?"

"Sonny, at my age, you get short of breath climbing the stairs to bed!"

I knew there was an airway between Toronto and Buffalo that went over Niagara Falls.

"Edgar," I said, "on these high altitude flights, do you ever see other airplanes?"

"Sometimes but they never bother me. They're usually underneath."

"Edgar," Eric said loudly and seriously, "I don't want you flying above 12,500. Do you understand?"

"Well you said I could if I got an instrument rating. How hard can that be? Them airline pilots get them all the time."

"It's a whole course, Edgar," I said. I knew I could talk him out of it by appealing to his wallet. "You have to take ground school classes, at least 40 hours of dual flight lessons and then write an exam and take a flight test."

"Okay," the little old man said to me. You could hear extra enthusiasm

95

in his voice. "It'll give me someone to fly with. Book me a lesson this time next month."

"That's the spirit," Eric grinned. "In four years of lessons you'll have the instrument rating." Eric liked the idea of an instructor flying with Edgar, especially if it wasn't him.

"See if you can lose some weight," Edgar said pointing at my stomach. "Otherwise we'll never get over 12,500!"

Chapter Sixteen

Elmer the snitch

Derry Air had a regular visitor who we code named "Elmer". He was an older man who drove into the parking lot in a stationwagon bristling with radio antennas. He never came into the flying school but after each of his visits, Angel received a request from the Department of Communication for copies of the Derry Air flight sheets for the day he was there. This would be followed by a letter to a Derry Air pilot citing him for non-standard radio procedures and warning about further transgressions.

The Derry instructors soon realized that there was a radio vigilante working the airport. We spotted him the next time he parked in our lot. He was hard to miss. The rusted, flesh-colored K-car looked like a cross between a Philippine taxi and a porcupine from outer space. Twin fibreglass CB antennas mounted on the back of the roof were bent forward and tied down. At least six other aerials of various shapes and sizes spiked the top of the car. Spot lights and clearance lights had been added to all corners. Reflective tape covered the rust holes. Mudguards and curb feelers were attached to the remains of the wheelwells. The licence plate was a "VE" call sign.

The Derry Airport was ripe for picking. The radio indiscretions cited in the letters from the government referred to lapses in the use of the phonetic alphabet for aircraft call signs. In reality, our radio procedures were a lot worse. The control zone was not very busy. Casual communication was the norm. The flying instructors at the two schools based on the field knew the air traffic controllers by name. Hamming it up on the radio relieved the boredom of circuits with students.

"Hey Shaky. I dated your sister last night."

"Good. We've been trying to pawn her off for years. She's yours now."

"She said we could live together... with you."

"Over my body."

At the next instructor meeting, Eric added the snitch to the agenda.

"In case you haven't heard, there is a radio 'do gooder' working our parking lot. If any of you see a light-colored stationwagon covered with radio antennas, let everyone know. I want to talk to this guy. In the meantime, use proper radio procedures or get reported. So far, the government has only issued warnings but if it keeps up, fines are next."

"What are the proper radio procedures?" Larry asked.

"In your case Larry," Eric replied, "don't use the radio. Let your students make all the calls."

"How are we going to get rid of this wiener?" Henry asked.

"The guy is probably a pilot wannabe," Eric replied, "but he is too shy to come into the flying school. This is his way of reaching out to the aviation community."

"No way, Eric," Henry said. "He's a born fink. I bet he lives with his mother and wears his pants up to his armpits. His Grade Three teacher would have picked him to hoist the Elmer Safety flag. He'd report his classmates for not looking both ways before crossing the street."

"Well, we could give him the benefit of doubt and invite him in for an introductory flying lesson."

"Only if you're going to drop him out of the airplane on his head," Henry said.

Eric ignored his remark. "We need to tell when he's here."

"We should be able to spot that car from the air," I offered. "Whoever sees him could use the code name 'Elmer'. We can pretend we're passing a message on the frequency."

"Good, 'Elmer' it is," Eric said. "Whoever spots him, sing it out."

The day "Elmer" came back, Larry was flying circuits with a student. He spotted the pink wagon and panicked. "Elmer! Elmer! Elmer!" he shouted over the frequency. "I mean, Tango Victor Hotel is downwind with Elmer for a touch and go."

"Tango Victor Hotel and Elmer are cleared touch and go," the controller replied.

Eric heard the call on the office monitor. He trotted outside and around the hangar to the parking lot. He told us later that there was a big guy sitting in the driver's seat of the K-car.

"The engine was idling," Eric said. "He saw me coming, jammed it into gear and floored the accelerator. He was gone in a hail of gravel."

"Face it, Eric," Henry said, "he's a nerd. The only reaching out he's doing is to make our lives miserable. We have to scare him off, permanently."

The next time Elmer cruised into the airport parking lot, Henry was flying with a student in the circuit. He spotted the snitchmobile sitting with it's engine idling. Smoke was puffing out of the old car's exhaust pipe.

"Derry Tower, this is Alpha November Delta," Henry transmitted, "there's a light-colored stationwagon in the general aviation parking lot and it's on fire. I suggest you dispatch the fire truck."

"Roger, Alpha November Delta. The truck is on its way."

Henry told us later that he watched from the downwind leg as the airport crash truck squirted out of the airport garages and headed for the lot behind the Derry Air hangar. It was the emergency truck with a swivelling cannon of a hose mounted above the cab.

The snitch had also heard the call-out. Henry said he was driving his wagon for all it was worth. "He was going out one end of the parking lot while the crash truck entered the other end. The wagon charged down the entrance road with fenders flapping and smoke belching out of its exhaust. He was pulling away from the truck."

"The fire-in-progress is getting away, November Delta," the controller said to Henry. "The fire boss wants to know if you saw any smoke other than the black exhaust."

"No," he admitted.

Elmer the snitch turned onto the county road. The fire truck stopped at the airport entrance.

We congratulated Henry on his imaginative thinking.

"It would have been fun to see the crash crew give him a shot from the hose," Henry said with a grin, "but I think he got the message."

Chapter Seventeen

Ice Patrol

Derry Air flew an ice patrol for the Seaway Authority. We had a contract to supply a pilot and an aircraft to fly around Lake Erie once a week during the winter.

Lake Erie is the shallowest of the chain of Great Lakes that provide shipping access to the interior of North America. It is the only big lake to freeze over. This forces the seaway to shut down for the coldest three months of the winter. The ice patrol flights provided historical records of the Lake Erie ice so intelligent predictions could be made of the future opening and closing dates of the waterway.

Each flight carried a photographer, an iceologist and a supervisor from the Seaway Authority. The contract called for a high-wing airplane, so we used the Cessna 172, the same one we flew for the highway patrol during the summer.

The flights were easy: fly one lap of Lake Erie at 1,000 feet just off the shoreline. Eric assigned a different instructor every week so each of us could enjoy the two-and-a-half-hour diversion from teaching students.

My first time to fly the patrol came in mid-January. Eric briefed me before the flight. "You fly counterclockwise around the lake from the right seat. The photographer sits in the left front because that window opens all the way up. Every ten minutes you slow the airplane to 80 mph and lift the left wing. The photographer opens the window and snaps a picture. The iceologist sits behind him with a chart, a board and crayons. He plots the ice thickness. The supervisor sits beside him and complains."

"How do they know the thickness of the ice?" I asked.

Eric smiled. "They say the colour of the ice tells them but Lake Erie is full of pollution so who knows? I think the whole contract is an excuse to go flying on an afternoon away from the office." The jolly chief instructor laughed. "I'd be surprised if there was film in the camera."

"Why does the supervisor complain?"

"He is naturally miserable. Complaining is the only thing he enjoys."

"Oh."

"You'll see."

On the day of the flight, the weather was cold but good. A two-inch snowfall the day before had covered everything with a fresh white blanket. There was a high ceiling of Cirrus clouds but it was clear below.

I was waiting at the flight desk when the three men from the Seaway Authority walked into the lounge. I introduced myself. "I'll be your pilot for the ice patrol today."

The iceologist was the first to accept my handshake. "Pleased to meet you," the big man said with a friendly smile. "I'm Peter. This is Helmut." He pointed to the man with the camera around his neck. I shook his hand. He nodded indifferently. He looked bored.

"And this is my boss, Sidley."

Sidley was a shrivelled up little man. "Pleased to meet you sir," I said. He took my hand and gave it one curt pump.

"This means we have yet another new pilot," he said. He injected considerable displeasure in his voice.

"Eric Daedalus has briefed me on the flight," I offered.

He wasn't listening. "So we have to train you on how to do this."

"The weather looks good," I said, trying to change the subject.

"I know," Sidley said. "We have a meteorologist."

"I've checked the airplane over," I continued. "I'm ready when you are."

The three men followed me out to the Cessna. Peter and Helmut were wearing parkas. Sidley was clad in a trench coat which was the wrong apparel if we had to walk home across the Lake Erie ice. I didn't have another coat to offer him, so I said nothing. The grumpy-faced little man climbed into the right rear seat first. This meant that I had to move my seat back against his legs to get in.

"Excuse me, sir."

"Just get in," he barked.

Before firing up the engine, I launched into a passenger briefing.

Sidley interrupted me. "We know, we know," he boomed. "You're the only one new on this flight remember. Now get going."

I finished the briefing. Peter smiled apologetically. Helmut stared out his side window.

I started the engine, called ground control, taxied out and took off. I climbed out to 1,000 feet and levelled off. We flew due south toward Lake Erie. No one spoke until I had crossed the shoreline and turned west. The lake appeared to be a solid frozen mass. The fresh snowfall had covered the surface. The only colour we were going to see on the ice was white.

"That's quite a change from last week," Peter said. "Last week we could see the bare ice surface."

"We're too close to the shoreline," Sidley bellowed over the engine noise. "I can't see the ice."

I let the Cessna drift further over the lake. Helmut turned toward me and held up his camera. I took that as a signal for a picture. I slowed to 80 mph. Helmut faced sideways, checked the airspeed indicator and unlatched the window. The slipstream flipped it up. The back seat was hit with an icy blast. Peter was ready. He held his lapboard in front of his face with a gloved hand. Sidley was not. I could hear him yelling over the roar of the wind. "You idiot! Tell me before you do that!"

I moved the left wing up. Helmut aimed his camera and fired. He reached up, pulled the window closed and latched it.

"Turn the heat up," Sidley demanded.

The heater knob was on full but I gave it a tug anyway.

We flew on in silence. The trip had to be a waste of time as far as meaningful data was concerned. The lake appeared to be a 200-mile uniform flat sheet of ice covered with snow. It was impossible to tell the ice colour and it was too early in the season for ice ridges to give away its thickness.

Ten minutes later, Helmut raised his camera. I reduced the power and raised the nose to slow us down.

"Window open," Helmut announced.

As soon as the words were out of his mouth, he released the latch. An icy blast swirled around the cabin. I rolled the left wing up. Helmut aimed and clicked.

As soon as he closed the window, Sidley yelled, "Turn the heat up."

"It's up all the way, sir," I replied, adding power.

We flew along in silence again. I could feel Sidley stamping his feet either from the cold or impatience or both. The heat slowly built up in the cabin. Before it got warm, it was time for another photo.

I didn't mind if the outing was a waste to the Seaway Authority. Except for the complaints from the pest behind me, I was enjoying myself. The great expanse of white made the flight challenging. Over the lake, there was no horizon for a visual reference. The high Cirrus layer blended the sky into the snow-covered ice. I compensated by dividing my attention between the aircraft instruments and the dark line of trees along the shoreline off to my right. This kept me busy between photo shoots.

After the next shot, Sidley issued another command. "Don't fly so high," he yelled. "I can't see anything from up here."

I was at 1,000 feet above the lake as outlined by Eric in his briefing. "You want to fly lower?" I shouted back.

"If I said we are too high, what did you think I meant?" the miserable man replied.

I looked at Helmut for guidance. The altimeter was in front of him. He turned and looked outside. I glanced back at Peter. He smiled but gave me no direction. I descended a couple of hundred feet.

A few minutes later, Sidley barked again. "We're too high. Take us down."

I dropped the airplane to 500 feet. When I had the Cessna trimmed level, we did another photo shoot. Afterward, Sidley continued to complain. "I don't know why you insist on flying so high," he yelled. "The contract calls for 1,000 feet. Fly lower."

I descended half the distance to the lake's surface using the altimeter for a reference. It was difficult to tell our height by looking at the expanse of white snow but I could see that we were nearly level with the shoreline.

"Lower," Sidley yelled impatiently. "I can't see anything from up here."

I dropped down to what I estimated to be 50 feet above the snow covered ice. This gave me a new reference. On our right, the dim shadow of our aircraft was following us on the surface.

"I still can't see anything this high up," the supervisor barked. "What's the matter with you?"

I half turned in his direction without taking my eyes off the instruments. "We're down to 50 feet, sir," I declared.

There was a short silence. "That's hogwash. I want to go down where I can see the surface and I want to do it now!"

Sidley must have been suffering from an illusion of altitude caused by staring at the unbroken expanse of white snow. I shoved the nose down and cut our altitude in half. I looked over at Helmut. He shrugged.

"Lower!" Sidley demanded.

The little man was bugging me. I could tell by our shadow that we were close to touching the surface. I checked my seat belt. It was tight.

"Lower it is!" I called back.

I pushed forward on the elevator control. Our shadow slid over and met us as our nosewheel bounced off the ice surface. "Thump!" The impact made a dull thud muffled by the snow. A puff of the white stuff sailed past the side window.

"What the..." Sidley exclaimed.

I looked at Helmut. He was smiling for the first time. I pushed forward again and thumped the nose wheel once more. The devil made me do it.

"I think we'll have to go back to Derry," Peter said tentatively.

This was met with silence. Then the smell rolled into the front of the airplane. Sidley had had an accident.

Chapter Eighteen

Attitudes and movements

Every year the government offered refresher courses for flying instructors. It sounded like a good idea: instructors together with the government aviation gurus reviewing the latest instructional techniques. It was better than instructors learning of changes in standards from angry students returning from failed flight tests, which is what happened the rest of the year.

I asked Eric for permission to apply.

"Why are you asking me?" the jovial pilot replied.

"Because if I'm accepted, I need a week off at our busiest time."

"There are a few things you should know," he said with a grin. "The Derry Air owner that we all know and love, Stingy Mingy, will grant you days off for a refresher course any time. He won't pay you but he's happy to give you the time off. The government never pulls base inspections at flying schools that have sent instructors to refreshers. Besides, the course is only five days. Angel will schedule you to work 10 days before and 10 days after, including the weekends. The course will be your time off for the month. The good news is that the government pays you and if you don't crash one of the airplanes, they'll renew your Instructor's Rating."

Despite Eric's insight, I was excited to be accepted on the course. I had never rubbed shoulders with government inspectors except during my own instructor flight tests. These were always one-way affairs with me demonstrating my instructional technique and the inspector telling me what I was doing wrong but not telling me what was right. Now I was going to learn from the masters.

"Would it deflate your enthusiasm if I told you that all applicants are accepted?" Eric asked. "No one has ever applied who has attended before so they can never get enough candidates."

"No," I replied.

"Have fun," he laughed.

The course was at a flying school in the town of Pie, an hour drive from Derry. I arrived at the classroom before the nine o'clock start time. A huge disappointment greeted me. The five-day course was being lead by Inspector Kennedy, my nemesis. Every time something had gone wrong during my flying career, Kennedy was involved. The crusty, gran-ite-faced government inspector probably said the same thing about me.

"Good morning, sir," I squeaked with a forced cheerfulness.

"You're lucky to be on this course," Kennedy grunted. His look and tone were sour. "We had a cancellation."

"How can I thank you?" I replied sarcastically.

"Sit down. The first class is about to start."

"Yes, sir."

I took a seat.

Kennedy began by introducing the two other inspectors running the course.

"Our schedule is basically the same every day: classroom work in the morning followed by lunch on your own and flying in the afternoon. There is a restaurant upstairs in the flying school for meals.

"To start off, I'd like each of you to stand, state your name and tell us where you're from."

There were 11 instructors from around the region. All but one other looked like teenagers. I suddenly felt ancient. I had been teaching flying for several years.

"This is an informal session," Kennedy said, trying to smile. He looked out of practise. "We are here to exchange ideas."

Excellent, I thought.

"To start, I'd like our instructor from Derry Air to come to the front and give the pre-flight briefing for the Attitudes and Movements lesson."

I was flabbergasted. I was here to learn, not teach. My letter of accep-tance had said "where" and "when" and to bring my instructor manuals. I was not prepared to give lessons.

"Don't be shy," Kennedy said. The whole class was looking at me. "You would be expected to do this on any given day at work as an instruc-tor."

He was right but it was the first lesson on the pilot course and one of the more difficult to teach. It was a dirty trick to ask me to present it with no warning. I stood up and slowly walked to the front of the class. Kennedy handed me a piece of chalk and then joined the other two inspectors sitting at the back of the room.

For teaching aids, there was a blackboard on the front wall, a generic high-wing model airplane and a cardboard-mounted picture of a Cessna

172 instrument panel on an easel.

I picked up the wooden model and started weakly. I haltingly described the three aircraft movements while gathering my thoughts on the lesson. I injected plenty of "umms" and "aahs". It wasn't going well but the young instructors sat quietly. The inspectors at the back began talking among themselves. They emitted the occasional burst of laughter. I tried to ignore them while describing the aircraft controls and movements with the model. I wasn't doing a good job.

It occurred to me that when I was done, Kennedy, the other inspectors and perhaps the whole class were going to critique my performance. I was giving them lots of ammunition for a bad review.

An inspector laughed loudly at something that was said at the back. The lack of courtesy bugged me. I stopped my lesson and put down the model. "I'm going to start the lesson over," I declared, "but before I do, the three of you at the back will have to shut up or leave the room."

They stopped talking. Several classmates gaped at me in horror. Others turned to see the reaction at the rear.

"That's better, thank you," I said. "Now my favourite way to teach this lesson is to relate it to life."

I launched into a version of Attitudes and Movements that I had seen a drunken Eric Daedalus perform at a pilot's stag one Saturday night in Derry.

"There are three movements to know when learning to fly," I said. "The first is pitching." As I spoke, I gyrated my pelvis out and in like a dog in heat. "Then there is yawing," I said while wiggling my hips Elvis-style left and right. "And rolling." I twisted my body both ways like Chubby Checker.

At the back of the room Kennedy's mouth was open but no sound was coming out. The other instructors were at various stages of smiling.

"There are four attitudes," I continued while dropping to the floor. I sat down, leaned back and thrust my pelvis in the air like a groom waiting for his bride to come out of the bathroom on the wedding night.

"The nose-up attitude..." There were a few giggles from the class. The two inspectors were looking at Kennedy. I flipped forward into a push-up position and pretended there was someone intimate underneath me. "...and nose-down attitude."

Kennedy stood up. "That's enough!" he barked. "Save the Tom Foolery for the barroom. Take your seat."

I got up willingly and went to my desk. He asked one of the other instructors to come up and teach the lesson. A red-faced youngster played it straight and gave us a halting, textbook version of the briefing.

"Very good," Kennedy said. He was talking to the instructor but he was glaring at me. Then Kennedy made some suggestions about using the instrument panel picture for that lesson. "If we had actual instruments discarded from the maintenance shop, we could use those," he added. "Of course we would have to make sure that they're properly tagged as unserviceable."

Kennedy then invited the class to comment on the lesson. No one did.

"Right then. We'll take a coffee break and come back to review straight and level flight, climbing, descending and turning."

The break was upstairs in the restaurant overlooking the airport. The inspectors sat in their own group. Most of the instructors buried themselves in books to review the upcoming lesson. The one "older" fellow came over and introduced himself.

"I'm Gerry Schneider," he said offering me a handshake.

Schneider was a gangly redhead about my age.

"You're from Kitchener," I said, shaking his hand.

"I teach in Kitchener," he said. "I'm from Alberta."

"That explains the cowboy boots. Pleased to meet you."

"Likewise," he said with a crooked smile. "I loved the briefing. I hope tonight we get to see the rest of it in the bar."

"Hopefully the bar is the only place I'll have to perform for the rest of this week."

His grin widened. "I think you can count on it."

Chapter Nineteen

Hydro slalom

The rest of the morning classroom sessions on the first day of the instructor refresher course followed the same pattern. An instructor was asked to demonstrate one of the ground briefings on the pilot's course. The government inspectors sat at the back of the classroom and picked the lesson apart.

Before the break for lunch, Kennedy announced the flying assignments for the afternoon. The host flying school had provided two, four-seat Cessna 172s and a Cessna 150 two-seater. Two government inspectors would fly the 172s with three instructors from the course. They would do three flights each covering the three lessons from the morning briefings, rotating pilots in the right front seat for each one.

Inspector Kennedy said he would take three more instructors in the government Beech Baron to give them a taste of multi-engine flying; three flights with a pilot rotation after each.

When names for all the seats had been called, Gerry Schneider and I were left over. Kennedy pointed at us. "You two will fly the Cessna 150 together," he said.

"Thank you sir," I replied insincerely. I had no idea what we were expected to do.

"Practise the morning lessons," he continued. "And don't come back until three hours are up."

During lunch, I thought I might have an opportunity to make up for my grandstanding in the morning session. I was planning to be nice to Kennedy but he and the other inspectors climbed into a government car and drove away. The cholesterol castle at the airport must have been below their expense allowance.

I sat with Gerry Schneider, the beanpole, redheaded cowboy who I had met during the coffee break. I found out that he, like me, had been instructing for a few of years. He seemed easygoing and likeable.

Gerry and I signed out the Cessna 150 after lunch. Walking to the airplane, he said, "Without an inspector, I guess we can do whatever we want."

"You're right. It's a bit of a waste being on our own but the weather's good."

"That takes some of the fun out of it, but we should find something interesting to do." His mouth was set in a mischievous grin.

At that moment I caught sight of the tail on the 150. It was painted in a checkerboard pattern. "Gerry," I said excitedly, "look at this. It's a Cessna Aerobat."

The airplane was the beefed-up version of the basic Cessna 150 trainer. For me, this placed a new perspective on the afternoon.

"I've never flown aerobatics in an aerobatic airplane," Gerry said.

"Until now," I replied.

His grin grew wider. "You go first," he offered.

I had the right partner.

We split a quick external inspection and jumped in. I took the instructor seat on the right. Gerry strapped into the left. He fired up the Continental engine while I worked the radios. I announced that we were taxiing for a local flight. We could see the other groups dutifully following the inspectors around the aircraft listening to detailed pre-flights.

Gerry flew the airplane from the takeoff into a climbout.

"Head away from the practice area," I said. "We don't want any witnesses."

"Okay partner," Gerry replied.

"Level off at four thousand five hundred feet," I continued, "and then I'll take control."

"Roger, dodger."

When it was my turn to fly, I looked around for other traffic. "I'm going to demonstrate the attitudes and movement lesson," I said. "Pull your seatbelts tight. What's the first movement?" I asked, treating him like a student.

"Pitching," he replied.

"Right." I shoved the control wheel forward. "There is pitching down...," our stomachs floated as the g load came off and the airplane built up speed, " ...and pitching up!" I hauled back on the control wheel and squeezed the right rudder pedal. We were pressed into our seats. The nose of the Aerobat zoomed skyward. I shoved the throttle in all the way.

"Yahoo!" Gerry whooped.

The airplane's speed bled off rapidly as we floated over the top of a loop. The horizon slid into view upside down. I pulled the power off to idle as the nose curved earthward. I increased the back pressure on the

112

elevators and the gs built up again. When the nose was pointed at the horizon, I restored the power and neutralized the elevators. The excess speed zoomed us back up to altitude.

"Okay, hotshot, it's student practice time. You try it."

We flew loops for nearly an hour. Gerry was a good pilot but it took him a few tries to find the ideal combination of entry speed, back pressure and power to milk the low-powered Cessna over the top.

On his first attempt, he didn't pull hard enough. The little airplane stopped flying when we were pointed straight up. This was followed by a brief tail slide and an almighty whip stall. Then the airplane snapped into a wicked spin.

"Whoa doggy!" Gerry yelped as the airplane corkscrewed earthward. "This doesn't look like the one you did." He initiated a spin recovery.

On his second try, we made it around further but the airplane stalled on its back and flopped over into another spin.

"Ride 'em cowboy!" he yelled. The spin tightened as he pushed the wrong rudder. "Which way is up?"

"I have control," I yelled.

Gerry lifted his hands off the wheel.

On his third try, he pulled too hard during the entry. The Cessna obligingly snaprolled to the left as we were pitching up. The sky rotated and both doors unlatched. We tumbled into a spin.

"You have control," Gerry bellowed. He held his hands up. His eyes were wide. "What was that!?"

I started a recovery. "I think you reinvented the Lomcevak," I replied with a laugh. "Next time, pitch up somewhere between the last two tries."

He got the hang of it. Each time around, his "Yahoos" grew louder.

"Let's take a break," he finally said.

"Okay, but we have to land somewhere other than Pie or Kennedy will not be pleased."

His face brightened up. "Let's go to my home base in Kitchener. It's not far. I'll buy the coffee."

"You're on."

Gerry found Kitchener and landed. When he shut down near the restaurant, he said, "I'll leave the master switch on and that'll keep the Hobbs meter running. If anyone questions the low tach time, we'll say that we practised everything at reduced power."

"Okay," I said.

Gerry showed me around the flying school. I met some of his co-workers and then we sat down for a coffee.

"What's next?" I asked.

"I'll show you how my instructor taught me attitudes and movements," the grinning cowboy said.

"Okay," I replied.

We walked outside and Gerry climbed into the right seat. He started the engine and worked the radios. After takeoff, he levelled off at 1,000 feet and flew over the city. On the other side of the built-up area, he pointed out a twin set of high voltage power lines running to the horizon. "Those head toward Pie."

"I see that."

Without saying any more, Gerry eased the Cessna's nose down. We descended until we were hedge-hopping beside the long row of towers. Gerry turned the airplane toward them. By the time I realized what he was doing, it was too late to stop him.

"The ailerons create the rolling movement," he instructed calmly. His face was split by a huge grin. The Aerobat slid under the wires between two sets of towers. "This is rolling left," he said. We passed out the other side about 10 feet above a farm field.

114

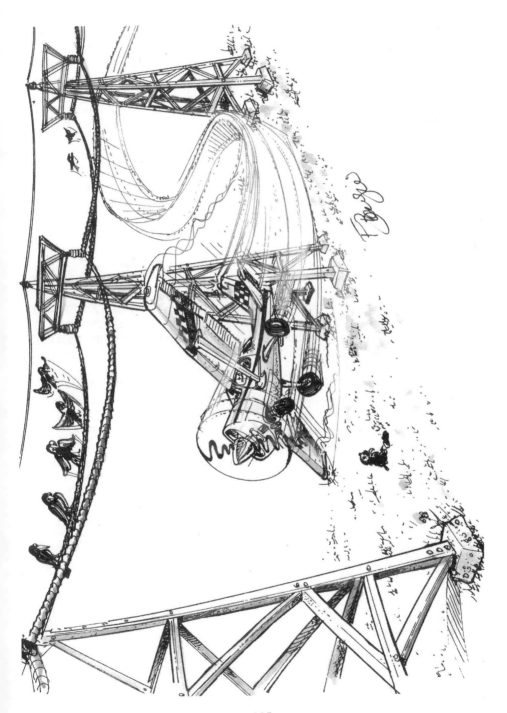

115

My mouth was open but no sound came out. Before I could recover, Gerry said, "And this is rolling right." The Cessna curved around the next set of towers and under the wires. "The further we turn the control wheel, the faster the airplane rolls." He rolled left.

It was terrifying but cleverly done. Gerry matched the standard first lesson patter with a series of interconnected turns. We zigzagged between each set of hydro towers under the lines. Occasionally he had to interrupt the flow of instruction to miss a barn or climb over a tree line.

"Student practice time," he announced, still weaving between the towers. "You have control."

I gripped the wheel and continued the slalom. I had no previous experience flying ultra-low. My chest ached from the intense concentration. My arms and legs twisted in knots trying to catch the rhythm of rolling back and forth while avoiding the hydro towers and every other obstacle in southern Ontario.

"Very good," Gerry said in a fatherly tone. "I have control."

"You have control," I said. I realized that I had been holding my breath the whole time that I had been flying.

"Now we can combine the different attitudes and movements," he said without breaking stride. "We can have a nose up attitude with a left bank." He pulled the nose up and rolled into a left turn over the top of the wires. "Or we could have a nose down attitude with a bank right." He shoved forward and turned right under the wires between the next set of towers.

We flew like that all the way to Pie. I was exhausted from fear and concentration by the time we landed. When we were walking in from the flight line, I asked, "Was your instructor a Kamikaze pilot?"

"No. He was a crop duster who taught flying in the winter."

"What else did he show you?"

"That's a lesson for another day."

Chapter Twenty

Water skiing

On the morning of the second day of the refresher course, instructors were again asked to demonstrate pre-flight briefings. The three government inspectors sat at the back of the classroom and critiqued the performances.

In the afternoon, nine of the instructors were split into groups of three. Two of the trios flew with inspectors in Cessna 172s for three hours practising the morning lessons. The third group flew with Inspector Kennedy in a Transport Canada Beech Baron for multi-engine instrument demonstrations. Gerry Schneider and I were left to fly by ourselves in the Aerobat again.

"So what's the agenda today?" Gerry asked. His face was set in a crooked smirk.

"Well, Kennedy thinks we're going to practise turns, climbs and descents," I replied. "It sounds like hammerheads to me. What are you teaching?"

"Straight and level flight," the redheaded cowboy replied.

"That's it - just straight and level flight?"

"Yah. My instructor taught it to me on the water."

"Water skiing?"

"Right," he replied. "You've done it?"

"Never! I've seen ag pilots ski the main wheels in their tail draggers but I can't imagine doing it in a Cessna 150."

"Very carefully, very carefully," Gerry grinned.

"I'll stay here and you can tell me about it if you make it back."

"No, no. It's as easy as standing on a flagpole. Besides, you have to teach me hammerheads."

We went flying. I demonstrated a hammerhead turn. They are difficult to do in a 150. The 100-hp engine runs out of steam quickly during the

pitch up. The initial pull has to be just right. Too little and there is
not enough momentum to rudder the airplane around before it slides
backward. Pulling too hard on the entry stalls the wings.

Gerry practised. After a series of slides, snaprolls and spins, he got it
right.

"Yahoo!" he hollered as the little airplane skidded around into a dive.
"Hammerheads should be added to the Private Pilot lessons. We covered
the first half of the whole course including stalls and spins in one
manoeuvre."

"Okay. I'll let you tell Kennedy."

"I don't think so."

"Ready for a coffee stop?" I asked.

"Sure. Where to this time?"

"Brantford's not far."

"Okay, Brantford it is."

We landed and had coffee at the snack bar in the Brantford Flying Club.

"Are you ready for a water skiing lesson?" Gerry asked with his trade-mark crooked grin.

Years earlier I had witnessed a formation of agricultural spraying air-planes being flown on the water. It was a late evening stunt flown on Lake Erie during an ag-pilot convention. The pilots touched their wheels on the smooth surface near the shoreline. I was watching from an airplane over-head. It was fun to see the twin lines being carved in the water by each set of tires. I never tried it. I never wanted to try it.

I pointed at the windsock. "Isn't it too windy to water ski?" I asked hopefully. "I know how to swim but I don't want to practise it in a Cessna 150."

"Out west we don't call it wind until it hits 25 mph. Trust me. It's not too windy."

I had trapped myself into doing whatever Gerry wanted. I had started the hair-brained variations and now it was his turn to top me. I was going to learn how to water ski a Cessna 150 from a prairie dog in cowboy boots.

"Okay captain. Whatever you say."

Gerry flew the takeoff from the Brantford Airport. He levelled off at 500 feet and headed southeast. "Small corrections in level flight are made using the pitching movement," Gerry explained as he lapsed into instruct-ing mode. "Rudder movements keep the airplane straight. I'll show you."

He pushed forward on the control wheel and dove toward the Grand River, a muddy waterway that snakes lazily through the flat land of south-ern Ontario. He hung the little Cessna just over the surface in reduced power level flight.

"The trick is to make the airplane work for you," he continued. "It's designed to stay in straight and level flight. All you do is help it using a light touch on the controls."

Trees along both riverbanks sheltered the surface from the wind. I could see that the water was smooth enough to ski but there were no straight sections. In some places, the Grand was only four or five wingspans wide.

Gerry was concentrating hard. I realized that he had stopped talking. He descended the last few feet in a slight nose up attitude and touched the main wheels to the surface. The Cessna slowed. Gerry added power and back pressure. Out of the corner of my eye, I could see spray coming off the left tire but I didn't turn to look directly at it. The right-hand shoreline of the curving river was filling the windshield. Gerry gently lifted the right wing and, with the left tire skiing on the surface, turned left. A small set of power lines flashed overhead. I saw them but I was too terrified to speak. The river turned right. Gerry eased the right tire back on the water and lifted the left one. We rounded the corner under another power line. Cool air flowed through the cockpit vents but Gerry was sweating from the concentration. My body fluids were accumulating in my bowels.

We skied around another bend.

"Bridge!" I yelled.

Gerry pulled the nose up. "Large changes to level flight are accomplished with a combination of pitch and power," he explained, pushing the throttle in.

We hopped over the bridge and dropped back down. Gerry continued the water dance of left and right turns following the winding river. It was a beautiful piece of airmanship but it was terrifying to watch from the cockpit.

"Boat!" I bellowed.

"Use the rudder to keep straight but heading changes are made with small turns," he said lifting the left wing over the heads of two men fishing.

"Okay, okay," I squeaked. "Now let's go home."

"Student practice," he replied calmly, popping over a small railway bridge. "You have control." He lifted his hands in the air.

I grabbed the wheel. There was a wider section of river ahead with only a gentle bend.

"It's a good exercise to teach gentle control corrections," Gerry said.

He was right. I thought I was a good pilot but the finesse required to keep one tire or the other on the surface eluded me. We went a long way before any wheels touched the water.

"This is low flying, not water skiing," Gerry said.

Then I forced both main tires in too hard. Their buoyancy popped us back into the air. This was followed by a series of hops and skips. Every time I thought that I might get it right I had to switch my concentration to fly under wires or pull up to avoid a bridge.

"Do you know anyone who flipped over trying this?" I asked. I was looking for an excuse to quit. I was suffering the double embarrassment of appearing petrified and showing my lack of piloting skill.

We skipped around a right-hand bend in the river and hopped over a swimming raft.

"The only problem I had doing this," Gerry commented, "was during solo practise as a student pilot. I met my flying instructor and another student coming the other way."

Chapter Twenty-one

Road circuits

On Day Three of the instructor refresher seminar we covered the ground briefings for takeoffs, landings and off-airport approaches. During lunch, my flying partner, Gerry "Cowboy" Schneider, asked what I was going to teach in the air.

"Takeoffs and landings," I replied, "how about you?"

"That's it? Takeoffs and landings?"

"Yup. But we'll do them at 4,500 feet, Bob Hoover style."

"All right!" he exclaimed. "I'll teach road circuits."

"Road circuits? I've never heard of them."

"You easterners think all off-airport landings are emergencies. I'll show you."

We went flying in the Cessna 150 Aerobat. I took the instructor's seat first. Gerry played student.

"Avoid the practice area and climb to 4,500 feet," I said to him.

When we reached altitude, I took control. "Pretend the ground is at 3,500 feet. We are on a downwind leg for a touch and go."

"Okay."

"Our objective is to see how many Bob Hoover touch and goes we can do without breaking through the 3,500-foot floor..."

"Whatever you say, partner."

"...with the engine off."

"Whoa baby! My guess is one. Maybe," Gerry said.

"Watch this."

I did a pre-landing check, pushed the nose down and turned on an imaginary base leg. The wind noise shrieked through the drafty airplane as the airspeed built up. When it reached the red line, I turned final and closed the throttle.

As we were approaching 3,500 feet, I hauled the nose up to the horizon and executed a barrel roll to the right. When the wings came around to level again, the nose was down and headed for the imaginary runway. We "touched" at 3,500 feet, I snapped the nose up and barrelrolled to the left. It was a slower roll but we were 300 feet above the "ground" when the wings came back to level. I held the nose down to 3,500, pulled it up and forced a roll to the right. The airplane staggered around slowly. As we were returning to level, we busted through the ground altitude by 200 feet.

"I guess Bob Hoover only did two," Gerry said with a grin.

"He had a different airplane," I replied. "Student practice," I said, gesturing for him to take control.

Gerry climbed the airplane to 4,500 feet. On his first roll, he didn't appreciate how much the control deflections in the basic trainer had to be exaggerated. Rolling through inverted, he didn't push forward enough. We came around in a steep dive, plunging through 3,500 feet at 150 mph.

Gerry's next try worked better but he didn't have enough momentum to complete the roll the other way. The Aerobat stalled out while inverted and flopped into a spin. He got two complete rolls on his third try.

I let him practise a few more and then asked, "Where's the coffee break this afternoon?"

"Simcoe."

"There's no coffee shop at the Simcoe Airport."

"The A&W up the street has coffee...and Lolita."

"Lolita?"

"Yah, she's the car hop. She's worth the stop."

"Okay."

We landed at Simcoe's grass strip, parked and walked a couple of hundred yards along the highway. The A&W restaurant was one of the old-style drive-ins with menus and speakers at each parking spot. There was no indoor seating.

Gerry walked up to the first speaker and pushed the signalling button. "Welcum to Hay and Wubboeyou," a girl's voice boomed through the tinny speaker. "Can I take youse ordda?"

Gerry whinnied like a horse. "Wheeeeeeeeh. Whoa there Trigger, hold your horses. G'morning ma'am. Two black coffees for my partner and me."

"Mista Gerry!" she squealed. "Eet's you. Hokay, comin' up, two bleck coffee right a-way!"

I was not prepared for Lolita. A large, middle-aged Latin dressed in a billowing orange-coloured, fruit-patterned dress came bursting out of the restaurant. She sashayed up the centre sidewalk enthusiastically swinging a serving tray over her head.

"Mister Gerry, Mister Gerry," she cried excitedly. "Eet's bin too long you come here, no?"

"Hi Lolita. It's good to see you."

As the Latin momma approached us, she swung the tray in front of her. "Oooah. You brought a friend. How nica to meet you. I'mma Lolita."

Gerry introduced us. "Pleased to meet you, Lolita," I said, looking at the tray. The coffee was in clear glass mugs. It looked like crankcase oil.

Gerry handed Lolita a five-dollar bill. "Keep the change, baby," he said. Lolita squealed in delight.

After two sips, I had had enough coffee for a week. Gerry finished his and we walked back to the airport. Gerry took the instructor's seat. "Okay, here we go," he announced, "takeoff and landing practise - western style."

We departed Simcoe's Runway 27 with Gerry flying. He climbed the Cessna to circuit height and flew straight out over the city. It was the last time we saw 1,000 feet for the rest of the lesson. There was a paved road on a county line running from Simcoe southwestbound. It went straight as far as we could see. As we left Simcoe behind, the number of houses and cars on the road thinned out quickly.

"Now you'll see why westerners learn to fly in the minimum time," Gerry said. He did a pre-landing check and set up an approach for a landing on the road while launching into the patter for a touch and go lesson.

"Man's worst invention was the mailbox," he added. "A Cessna 150 wing will clear most of them but once in a while, a homeowner with an overloaded ego will build a roadside monument to himself just for the

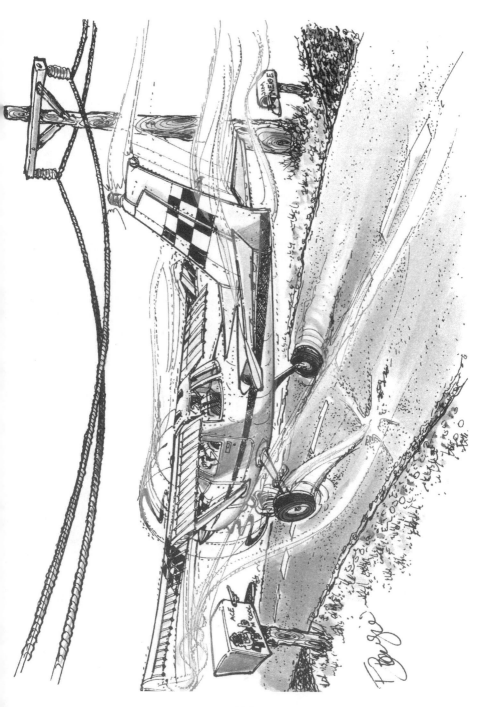

mail."

He cut the power, flared out and touched down.

"What about hydro wires?" I asked staring at a power line crossing the road ahead.

"Predictable," he replied calmly. "On this road the hydro runs on the left side, so a wire crosses the road every time there's a house or farm on the right."

He let the Cessna coast under the wire. The wing tips just cleared the poles on either side. He applied full power and demonstrated a takeoff.

In the space of five miles Gerry did a series of touch and goes, and stop and goes covering regular, short and soft field takeoffs and landings. He deftly hopped over or under hydro wires and lifted one wing or the other over tall mailboxes and road signs. He delayed his approaches when a car was coming.

"Have you every gotten in trouble doing this?" I asked.

"No, but I obey the rules of road circuits."

"What rules?"

"The three rules of road circuits are:

1/ Always use a road near another airport. It makes their phone ring instead of yours.

2/ Don't use the same road twice in one week. The cops'll wait for you to come back but they give up after a while.

3/ Give way to Mennonite buggies."

"You have a soft heart for Mennonites?"

"I do after seeing what happens when one of their horses comes face-to-face with an airplane."

Chapter Twenty-two

April fool to you too

Day 4 of the Instructor Course was April 1. It was also our turn to fly with Inspector Kennedy in the Baron. All week, Kennedy had been demonstrating multi-engine instrument flying procedures in the government aircraft. This had been a treat for the other course participants but Gerry Scheinder and I had flown twin-engine aircraft and already held instrument ratings.

"I have already done the pre-flight inspection," Kennedy said as we walked out to the airplane. There had been no pre-flight briefing. "I will be the pilot-in-command," the sour-faced civil servant continued. "You will observe only and not touch anything."

"Yes sir!" we chimed together.

"Mr. Schneider, you will ride in the front seat first."

Kennedy climbed into the Beechcraft and slid over to the left seat. I got into the back. Gerry followed, sitting in the right front. Kennedy ignored us both as he went through the start procedure and announced on the radio that he was taxiing for a local flight north.

I looked around the Baron. It was a nice airplane. There was none of the chipped paint, ripped upholstery and oil streaks that were the trademarks of the working airplanes that I had flown.

Kennedy took off without saying anything further to us. It was a clear day with just a little afternoon turbulence. The inspector turned north toward London, Ontario. The airplane climbed quickly. We were soon level at 4,500 feet cruising at nearly 200 mph. I couldn't help thinking that it would be a treat to fly an airplane like this.

Kennedy called London Tower and got permission to simulate a straight-in instrument landing system approach to Runway 32 followed by a full practice ILS to Runway 14. He intercepted the centreline localizer while still at 4,500 feet and lined up with the runway several miles back.

When he had captured the glideslope, Kennedy completed a pre-landing check, dropped the landing gear and followed the needle down.

The inspector flew smoothly and methodically. The needles on the course deviation indicator stayed crossed in the centre during the descent. He was obviously enjoying his demonstration.

The scenario was bugging me. We were burning 30 gallons an hour of taxpayer fuel so "old granite face" could practise instrument flying on a clear day while we sat silently. I leaned well forward pretending to get a closer look at the instruments. The Baron dipped its nose slightly. Kennedy eased the control wheel back before the glideslope needle showed the change. As the nose came up, I leaned back in my seat. The Baron continued to pitch up. Kennedy caught it but not before the needle twitched down. Gerry saw what I was doing. Kennedy didn't.

As the inspector corrected down, I moved forward. So did Gerry. He pretended to look for traffic ahead. The Baron dropped. The glideslope indicator moved up. Kennedy chased it.

This time I released my seat and rolled it back. So did Gerry. Kennedy caught the movement out of the corner of his eye. Gerry froze. The indicator dropped. Kennedy stabbed the nose down. I tracked my seat forward. Gerry bent over pretending to retie a shoelace. The Baron obeyed all three of us and dropped through the glideslope.

We crossed inside the outer marker. The glideslope needle deflections increased as the indicator got more sensitive. Gerry and I got more active. Kennedy got less smooth.

He managed to keep the needles from going to full deflection but he had to work hard to counteract the passenger-induced gyrations. He fought the Baron to the minimum approach altitude and commenced an overshoot.

"Simulated ILS to Runway one four approved Gulf Oscar," the controller said. "Call by the London Beacon outbound."

"Gulf Oscar."

Gerry and I stayed quiet and did nothing while Kennedy levelled the Baron at altitude. He crossed by the beacon outbound and flew a procedure turn. The localizer came alive. Kennedy turned in to line up with Runway 14. Just before the glideslope needle dropped toward the centre Gerry and I went to work. I slid from the left rear seat to the right. Gerry eased his foot forward and squeezed the right rudder pedal. The Baron dipped its right wing. Kennedy picked it up with the ailerons. Gerry pushed harder on the rudder pedal. I reached into the baggage compartment behind me and slid a box of Transport Canada training pamphlets over to the right side. Kennedy applied more left aileron control to keep the Baron on the centreline. The glideslope needle descended into the centre donut.

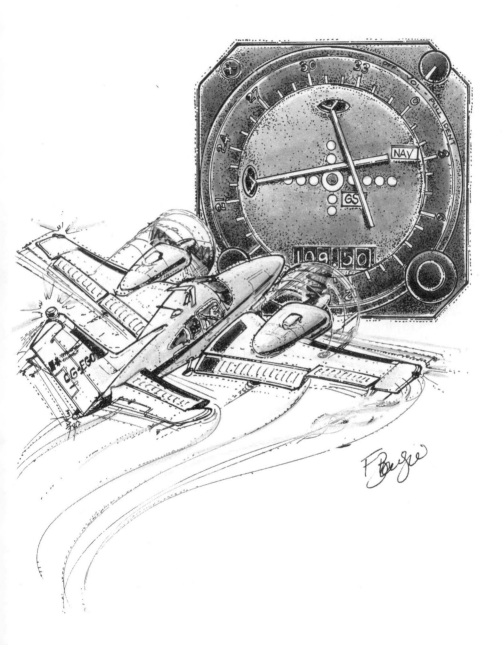

Gerry turned his head toward me and nodded. I slid over to the left side dragging the box in the back with me. Gerry took his foot off the rudder pedal. The Baron obediently skidded and rolled left.

"What the...!" Kennedy exclaimed.

The localizer needle jogged to the right. The inspector turned the airplane toward it. The glideslope indicator dropped out of the centre. I moved myself and the box to the right side. The Baron over-banked. Kennedy jerked it back. He popped his head up to see the runway for a second. Gerry swiped his hand over the left throttle and knocked it out of synchronization. The change in engine sound distracted Kennedy further. The Baron turned left. I slid over to the left seat and rolled it forward. I reached into the baggage compartment and pulled the box toward me. At the same time Kennedy shoved the nose down to chase the glideslope. The ADF indicator swung around to the tail indicating that we were crossing the beacon inbound. Kennedy's approach was going to hell in a handbasket.

"Want me to try it?" Gerry asked him loudly.

"No!" Kennedy barked as he kangarooed down the glideslope. His face was getting redder by the second. "Don't touch anything."

"How about gear down?" Gerry persisted.

I thought the veins were going to pop right out of the side of Kennedy's head. He shoved the propeller and throttle levers forward and grabbed the microphone. "London Tower, Echo Gulf Oscar, on the overshoot."

"What are your intentions, Echo Gulf Oscar?" the controller asked calmly.

"Straight out. We're returning to Pie."

"Straight out approved. What altitude are you climbing to?"

"Two thousand feet."

"Call level Gulf Oscar."

"Gulf Oscar."

Gerry and I sat quietly until Kennedy sorted everything out.

"How about a single-engine NDB approach at Pie?" Gerry suggested.

"The demonstration is over," Kennedy grumbled.

"Oh," Gerry replied. "Well, it was interesting. I learned a lot more than I expected," he said with a smirk. "I always thought Baron's were easy to fly."

No answer.

"Have you been flying for long?" he asked the lifetime pilot.

At this point, I thought that Gerry was pushing things a little too far with the stern inspector.

"Are we going to switch seats at Pie," Gerry persisted.

"The demonstrations are over," Kennedy replied solemnly.

"Oh, I thought we got three hours like everyone else."

Silence.

Gerry gave up. Kennedy flew a methodical visual approach to Pie's Runway 27. His procedures were once again flawless. He smoothly rolled the Baron onto a final leg, slowed down and set up for a landing.

"Want me to lower the wheels for you?" Gerry suddenly asked as he reached for the landing gear lever.

Kennedy jumped in his seat. His seat belt kept him from banging his head on the ceiling. His eyes locked on the three green lights.

"Gotcha!" Gerry declared enthusiastically. "Just kidding."

Kennedy had to chop the engine throttles to salvage his approach. It was not a good landing.

"Whoa baby," Gerry quipped as Kennedy brought the airplane under control on the runway.

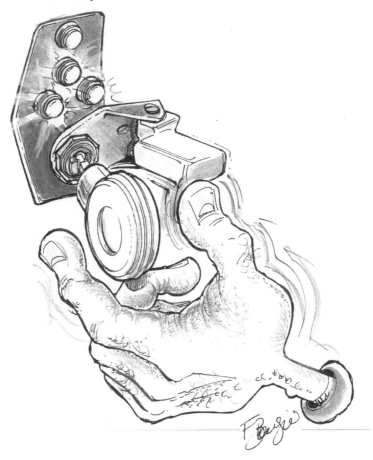

Kennedy got the last laugh. At the end of the course, the dark-suited inspector called the instructors forward one at a time, congratulated them and handed them one-year extensions to their instructor ratings along with an honorarium cheque. Gerry and I were last. He handed us each a cheque.

"What about our rating renewals?" I blurted out, staring at a cheque for $25.

"That's for instructors who demonstrated lessons with inspectors. Good day, gentlemen."

Chapter Twenty-three

To Indy or bust

Derry Air owner Irving Mingy asked if I would fly as copilot on a trip to Indianapolis. There was a charter for area sports reporters to the 500-mile auto race. Mingy picked me because I was booked off that day. He knew he wouldn't lose instructing revenue. He also knew I'd do anything for multi-engine flying time.

"Would you like a free trip to the Indianapolis 500 with Perry in the Navajo?"

When Mingy said, "free," it meant "no pay" but I was a race fan and had never been to "The Indy."

"Yes sir!"

"Be here at seven. It's an eight o'clock departure."

"Thank you, sir."

I told Eric about the offer. "I'm finally going to the big race."

"Not to dampen your enthusiasm," Eric said, "but I flew that trip one year. I couldn't get a ticket into the track. I watched the race on TV in the airport pilot lounge with Perry snoring beside me."

"I'll find a way," I replied.

I'd flown with Perry Butcher before. He was Derry Air's one and only staff charter pilot. Copilots for the Navajo flights were picked from instructors hungry for time in a larger airplane. Perry was burly, surly and insolvent. His bad temper had left him with a string of ex-wives and alimony payments.

When I arrived at work on the race day morning, Huey, Duey and Louey were pulling the Navajo out of the hangar with the old gray tractor. I walked into the office. Angel was there but there was no sign of Perry.

"Good morning Angel."

She hoisted two leather satchels onto the flight desk. "Here're the flight bag, minibar, logs and a credit card. Sign for them."

"Okay. Where's Perry?"

"It's too early," Angel replied. "I filed your flight plan. There's a copy in the bag. U.S. customs will meet the airplane at Indianapolis."

"Ah, thanks," I replied.

I signed a check sheet for the items she handed me and carried them out to the airplane. Huey was arranging the seat belts in the cabin, Duey was cleaning the outside of the windshield and Louey was fuelling the left wing.

I yelled at Louey over the noise of the pumper truck. "Do you know what Perry wants for a fuel load?"

"Angel ordered the fuel," he shouted back.

I nodded my reply and slung the bags onto the cabin floor. Huey carried them forward for me. I asked him if he had seen Perry, yet.

He looked at his watch. "It's too early," he replied.

I decided to do a walkaround. I had never done a pre-flight inspection on a Navajo so I just checked that the tires weren't flat, there was no fluid dripping from the engine nacelles and there was no evidence that the linecrew had rashed the wings or tail. I opened the oil access door on the left engine.

"I checked the oil," Duey offered. He was cleaning the windshield beside me. "Both sides are good."

"Thanks, Duey. Since I don't know what I'm looking for, I'll take your word for it." I closed the hatch.

"I put coffee on board," Huey said, climbing down the airstair door from the cabin.

"Thanks," I replied.

I walked around the rest of the airplane, entered the cabin and went forward to the cockpit. The Navajo was a flying instructor's dream. There were more dials and radios in front of each pilot than in any aircraft that I had flown before. I climbed over the flight bag and eased myself into the right seat. The big control yoke had an airliner feel to it. I hauled out the maps for the route and folded them onto my clipboard. I was refamiliarizing myself with the cockpit equipment when Huey stuck his head in the door.

"Passengers arriving," he declared.

"Thanks, Huey." I scrambled out of the seat. "Where's Perry?"

The lineman checked his watch. "Too early."

I went into the office. Six casually dressed men and one woman were at the flight desk. Angel was recording their names and handing them U.S. customs forms to fill in.

"This is one of your pilots," she said, pointing to me.

I introduced myself. The seven passengers were sports reporters from the local newspaper, radio stations and Derry's one TV station.

"Pleased to meet you," one of them said. "I'm Mike the Spike Windy."

I recognized his name as the sports reporter from the Derry Daily. He looked like a chesterfield jock - loud and round. He appeared to be the leader of the group. "What's our flying time to Indy?" he asked.

"Two hours and ten minutes," Angel replied from behind him in her flat monotone voice. "You can board the aircraft as soon as you complete these forms for U.S. customs. There are washrooms down the hall, if you need them. There are no facilities on the aircraft."

"New pilot and same friendly receptionist," Windy announced to no one in particular. Angel didn't smile. "Okay. Forms and then defuel," Windy said.

The group filled in the customs sheets with help from Angel and me and then headed down the corridor.

"Where's Perry?" I asked Angel.

"He'll be along. You board the passengers, do their briefing and wait for him."

"Okay."

I led the group out to the Navajo.

"Is this your first flight?" Windy asked with a laugh.

"First flight to the race," I replied. "I'm looking forward to it."

They climbed in and found seats. I shuffled up the narrow aisle and turned to face them from between the cockpit seats. Windy was in the first seat behind the pilots across from the galley. I pointed out the exits and the minibar.

"Where's the pretty stewardess?" Windy asked.

"I'll be serving refreshments once we get underway," I replied.

"Coffee, tea or me," Windy boomed.

Past the doorway, I could see Louey leading Perry toward the airplane. He appeared to be in his pajamas. As he got closer, I could see he was wearing a dirty pair of mismatched sweats. Wisps of his thinning dark hair were sticking out in all directions. Louey helped him onto the airstair door. When he was in, he closed it behind him.

Perry hauled himself up the aisle. I could see that he hadn't shaved. I turned around and sat down in the copilot's seat. It looked like he was ignoring me but it was hard to tell. His eyes were just slits in a puffy face. He was the picture of the morning after the night before. As he leaned into the cockpit, it was obvious that he hadn't washed or brushed his teeth.

Perry tentatively lifted his left leg over the captain's seat. His left hand reached for the engine magneto switches. He sagged down onto the cushion with his right leg still in the cabin. Without looking outside, he started the right engine. Then he pulled his right leg into the cockpit and started the left engine. Without doing up his seat belt, he donned a headset and

called Derry Ground Control. His voice sounded like his throat was full of broken glass. There was no reply from the controller.

I flipped the radio master switch on and set the ground frequency. The slit of Perry's right eye followed what I was doing. It was his first acknowledgement of my presence. He called again. The controller responded with taxi instructions and said our instrument clearance was on request. Perry released the brakes and headed us toward the runway. When the controller came back with our clearance, Perry growled that he was ready to copy. A rapid-fire clearance was issued. I wrote it down on my kneeboard. When Perry didn't respond, I punched my transmit button and read it back.

"Clearance correct, Delta Echo Romeo Yankee. Call the tower when you're ready for takeoff."

I acknowledged, changed the number two transmitter to the tower and set the transponder code. I switched the number one radio to the frequency for Toronto Centre.

Perry did about ten seconds of pre-take-off checks and then told the tower that he was ready. We were cleared to go. I madly looked around the cockpit to see if there was anything that we had missed.

Perry pulled onto the runway and applied full power. The Navajo meandered back and forth down the runway and took off.

"Switch to Toronto Centre now 133.3," the controller said.

Perry made no motions to respond.

"133.3, roger," I replied.

I turned the transponder on, switched to the centre frequency, raised the landing gear and set climb power on the throttles. I dialed in the first VOR frequency, routed it to Perry's side of the panel and then reached over and set his horizontal situation indicator to the course. The only indication that Perry was still awake was that he turned the aircraft to follow the indicator.

I continued handling the radio calls which were frequent. Not far south of Derry we were passed to American controllers. Perry climbed the Navajo to our assigned altitude of 8,000 feet, levelled off, turned the autopilot on and fell asleep. I knew he was sleeping because his head slumped against the side window, his mouth opened and he snored.

The autopilot followed the course and held the altitude. We were nicely skimming along on top of an undercast. When we passed the first VOR transmitter, I reached over and set the new course on Perry's HSI. I knew we could fly like this all the way to Indianapolis but I had other things I wanted to do. At the next frequency change I asked the controller if I could go off the channel for a few minutes to check the weather.

"Approved Echo Romeo Yankee. Call back by the Youngstown VOR."

"I'll call you by Youngstown, Romeo Yankee."

I took my headset off, unfastened my seat belt and stepped back into the cabin. I wanted to catch the organizer before he dozed off. He was slumped in his seat and his eyes were closed.

I squatted beside him. "How's it going back here?" I asked loudly.

He opened one eye. "Fine, fine," he replied.

I reached for a Styrofoam cup from the galley. I half filled the cup with coffee and then added an ounce of rum along with cream and sugar.

"I made some special coffee for you," I said loudly. I held the cup under Windy's nose. He took it. "Anyone else?" I asked. There were a couple of takers. The rest wanted to sleep.

Windy took a sip. Within a few seconds, the colour rose in his face. "This is good," he smiled.

"Glad you like it," I replied. "When you want more, just tap me on the shoulder."

I returned to the cockpit and reported back to the centre controller.

Every twenty minutes or so, Windy tapped my shoulder, smiled and held up his empty cup. I repeated the off-frequency routine and added a little more rum each time.

"Great coffee," Windy grinned.

Five coffees later, we were approaching Indianapolis. I poured a straight black coffee for Perry, nudged him awake and held the cup in his face. He took it. I pointed to our position on the map. He nodded.

The radio traffic was heavy. It sounded like every corporate and charter aircraft was converging on the race city. When the centre controller cleared us for an initial descent, he said, "Do not acknowledge any further transmissions. Change to Indianapolis Approach. Do not call."

Perry snapped off the autopilot and started us down. I changed frequencies in time to hear Indy Approach calling us with a radar vector that turned us 90 degrees. He ended the transmission with, "Keep the speed up. Do not acknowledge."

Perry turned on the new heading. I pulled out the approach chart book and listened to the automatic terminal information service. The controller continued vectoring a huge number of aircraft using a rapid-fire delivery and an open microphone. Each new aircraft contacted was told, "Keep the speed up. Do not acknowledge."

We were all being vectored around to line up to the parallel runways at Indianapolis International Airport, 23 Right and Left. We were in cloud so we couldn't see anything but it sounded like the controller was jamming a lot of aircraft into a small piece of sky.

"Maintain 160 knots, Delta Echo Romeo Yankee and switch to Indy Approach on one two seven one five. Don't call."

I changed frequencies and the controller was clearing us down to 3,500 feet. "Keep that speed up, Delta Echo Romeo Yankee. I need 160 knots to the runway. You are following a Falcon and there is a Gulfstream behind you. Do not acknowledge."

We broke out of the overcast at 4,000 feet. The Falcon was less than three miles ahead. The visibility was a little hazy but good. I picked out three more aircraft in front in a 10-mile space. I looked to the left. We were flying in formation with a parallel line of aircraft a half mile away.

The controller continued his open mike commentary. He was switching the traffic over to Indianapolis Tower ten miles from the runway. Perry held the power on and the speed at 160 knots. He looked like he was hurting but he was awake.

"Echo Romeo Yankee, you're ten back, keep the speed up and go to tower now. Don't call."

I had the tower frequency already selected on the other radio. I flipped the switch. "Delta Echo Romeo Yankee, you're number four to the Falcon. Maintain 160 knots. Expect to land with traffic on the runway."

From the controller's tone, if we didn't like how he was packing them in, we could overshoot and it would buy us vectors back to Derry.

I looked at Perry. He spoke for the first time. "When I call for the gear, dump it," he growled.

"Okay," I replied.

I could see the airport now. Traffic landing on the parallels was scooting onto the taxiways and heading to the cross runway at the far end. It had been turned into a mile-long aircraft parking lot.

"Cleared to land, Echo Romeo Yankee. Check the Falcon on short final, wind 200 at 10. Contact Indianapolis Ground point niner off the runway. Don't call and don't acknowledge. Gulfstream Zero One Bravo Mike, you're number three behind a Navajo."

Perry continued the approach at 160 knots. On short final he shoved the props into full fine pitch. The revs roared up to the red line and the airplane started to slow down. Then he chopped the power. The engines popped and sputtered.

"Dump it!" Perry barked. He pulled open the cowl flaps and then cocked the airplane in a full forward slip.

Windy liked that one. He was well liquored by now. "Ride 'em cowboy!" he roared from the back.

I yanked the landing gear down. We skated over the runway at 120 knots. Perry straightened the airplane, held it momentarily and then wheeled on the main gear. With the nose up slightly, he squeezed the brakes, expertly increasing the pressure as the speed dropped. We exited the runway at 45 knots.

"Well done, Exlax," I said with a smile.

"Whahoo!" Windy howled behind us. "The race is on and we're in first!"

I switched to ground control.

"Keep your speed up, Delta Echo Romeo Yankee. Follow the Falcon to parking."

Our speed stayed at 45 knots as Perry kept pace with the jet ahead. We zoomed onto the parking runway and slowed down. Ground crewmen with orange paddles were orchestrating a dance of big dollar aircraft. They herded them into twin rows down each side of the runway like elephants in a circus.

"Customs will meet your aircraft, Romeo Yankee," the ground controller said. "Welcome to Indy."

A paddle man on the run directed us to pass behind him and swing around counterclockwise into the line at an angle facing out.

I climbed out of my seat with the stack of U.S. Customs forms that Angel had given me. "As soon as the customs officer has cleared us," I announced to the passengers, "we'll arrange transportation for you to the terminal area."

I worked my way to the back and opened the airstair door. A ground crewman wheeled up in a golf cart. "Goodmorning. You need fuel and transportation?" he asked.

"Affirmative on both," I replied, "but we need customs first."

He snapped a walkie-talkie from his belt and spoke into it. Then he handed me a form. "Customs is on the way. Fill in this fuel request. We'll get a van for your passengers."

"Thank you."

I sidestepped up the aisle, handed Perry the fuel form and turned to my passengers. "Customs is on the way. Would anyone like a coffee while we're waiting?"

"Thought you'd never ask," Windy boomed. His speech was loud and slurred.

I poured him a 50/50 mix of rum and coffee. "There you go."

"You're a good man," he replied taking the cup.

"Thank you. By the way, would you happen to have an extra pass for the race?"

Windy knocked back the contents of the cup. Then he dug into his jacket pocket and came up with a fist full of media passes. "Take your pick," he offered.

I snatched one. "Thank you very much. I'll get you another drink, er coffee."

"My pleasure," he replied.

I poured him another coffee cocktail. A customs vehicle pulled up beside the airplane. A van and a fuel truck arrived in front. I greeted the customs official at the door. He climbed onto the first step and stuck his head in the cabin.

"All Canadians?" he asked.

"Yes sir," I replied. I handed him our paperwork.

He looked the cabin up and down, counted the forms and said, "Enjoy the race." He jumped off the stairs and was gone.

"Okay folks, the van is here. Grab your stuff."

I climbed down the stairs and waited as each passenger exited the airplane. I motioned for them to walk around the left wing to the vehicle. "We'll see you back at the terminal building after the race. Have fun."

Windy was the last out. I had to help him down the steps. I led him to the van.

I was determined to get to the race, but I stopped short of climbing into the van and leaving Perry with the airplane. I closed the sliding door and waved the van driver to depart.

As I turned around, I could see that Perry was climbing out of the airplane. His sweat pants were twisted one way, his shirt the other. His hair stuck out except where the headset had matted it down in a band from ear to ear. He held the coffee cup I had given him in one hand and the fuel sheet in the other.

The refueller approached me. "Do you have a fuel request?" he asked.

"The captain has it," I replied.

He hustled toward the cabin right past Perry who was ambling in my direction.

"Say, thanks for the help," he said. His voice was low and gravelly but he sounded sincere.

"You're welcome."

"I owe you."

"Well, there's a way you can pay me back."

His face immediately frowned. He lifted one eyebrow. "How's that?" he asked suspiciously.

"Look after the airplane and get us ready for the return flight so I can go and watch the race."

"You'll never get a ticket."

I pulled the media pass from my pocket.

"Go for it," Perry said.

Chapter Twenty-four

To catch a snitch

"If we can catch him doing something wrong, maybe we can scare him off permanently."

The speaker was Larry. The subject was "Elmer the snitch." This radio vigilante monitored the Derry Control Tower frequency and reported deviations from correct radiotelephone procedure to the authorities. This included most of the transmissions made by Derry Air pilots. We had scared him off for a week or two but he was back.

"Maybe the controllers will help us fish him in," Larry continued. "Then we'll ask Officer Shirley to put some fear into the guy."

The conversation was around the coffee pot on a bad weather day. The Derry Air instructors listened as Larry outlined his plan.

When he was done, he said, "I'll talk to the tower staff. Eric, you set it up with Shirley."

"Okay."

The next time that Elmer's stationwagon was spotted in the airport parking lot, the plan was hatched.

Larry went out to one of the airplanes parked on the Derry Air ramp, turned the master switch on and radioed on the ground control frequency. "Derry Tower, Golf Romeo Alpha Bravo, do you read?"

He had invented the aircraft registration. It was a code prearranged with the controllers."

"Aircraft calling on Derry Ground," the controller replied, "you're breaking up. Say again."

Larry repeated the call. His readability was five out of five.

"I can't make that out," the controller said. "Try another radio or microphone."

"Derry Ground, how do you read now?"

"Whoever is calling, it's all garbled. You'll have to get it fixed before you go flying."

"Derry Ground, Golf Romeo Alpha Bravo, I'm circling outside the control zone. I was unable to raise you on the tower frequency. I'm a student pilot low on fuel. Can you read me?"

"Airplane calling ground, you're still unreadable. Try another airplane or call us on the telephone."

While this was going on, Eric phoned police headquarters and asked to be patched through to Officer Roger Shirley. Roger was the cop who flew with Derry Air on the highway patrol. Between flights, his beat was the area around the airport.

"Operation Elmer is on," Eric told him when they were connected.

Outside, Larry was playing out the game. "Is there anyone else on this frequency who can hear me?" he asked. There was no reply. "If there is anyone listening who can hear Golf Romeo Alpha Bravo, please reply. I need to get this aircraft down."

Elmer heard the calls on his monitor. He picked up a microphone in his car and pressed the transmitter. "Derry Ground. It's Golf Romeo Alpha Bravo trying to call you on this frequency. He's a student pilot low on fuel trying to reenter the control zone. I can hear him if you want me to pass a message."

"Who's calling Derry Ground?" the controller asked.

"It's Golf Romeo Alpha Bravo calling Derry Ground. I can relay your transmissions."

"Derry Ground," Larry said. "It's Golf Romeo Alpha Bravo trying to get back to the airport."

"Aircraft calling Derry Ground, you're still unreadable. You can't fly in this control zone until you get that radio fixed!"

"Derry Ground," Larry pleaded, "I have to land."

No reply.

"Derry Ground," Elmer the Snitch said, "Golf Romeo Alpha Bravo has to land."

"Golf Romeo Alpha Bravo," the controller replied, "I read you five now. If you want landing instructions, call the Tower frequency."

"I can't raise the tower," Larry said.

"He can't raise the tower frequency," the Snitch said.

"I got two on at once," the controller said, "one readable and the other not. Who's calling Derry Ground?"

At that moment, Roger Shirley's police cruiser was coasting up behind Elmer's wagon. He stepped out dressed in his uniform complete with a swinging night stick and walked up to the open driver's side window.

"Okay buddy, let me see your licence to operate that radio," he barked.

Elmer jerked in his seat in surprise. Roger leaned toward the window and shook his baton. "It's a federal offence to operate a radio on aeronau-

tical frequencies without proper authority," he said. "Have you got a radio licence to show me?"

Elmer dropped his microphone and reached for his back pocket.

"Easy does it," Roger said, rapping his stick on the door.

Elmer slowly produced his wallet and extracted an Aeronautical Radiotelephone Operator's Certificate.

"I'll have to check this out," Roger growled and walked back to his cruiser. He ran the name through headquarters. Then he arranged to be patched through to Derry Air.

"Angel. Let me talk to Eric.

"So I've got this guy and he's licenced and clean. Now what do you want me to do?"

"You're the cop. Don't you know how to scare people?"

"I can't shoot him without a worse offence than talking," Roger replied.

"Well, give him a warning about transmitting on aircraft frequencies or something."

"Okay."

Roger went back to Elmer's car and waved his radio licence at him.

"This is for aircraft communications. This isn't an airplane, Mr. Osar Tenfor. I suggest you stay off the aeronautical frequencies until you're in the air. I'm going to let you off this time, but I don't want to catch you yakking at airplanes again unless you're in one. Understand?"

"Yes sir."

"Good." He handed his licence back and bid him a good day.

Roger drove off. So did Elmer.

It wasn't long before we heard from the Snitch again. Larry was in the lounge between flights when an overweight, middle-aged man walked in carrying a shoebox. He was wearing a sweatshirt and mismatched sweatpants. The bottoms were pulled up halfway to his armpits. A pair of thick heavy-rimmed glasses dominated his round face. They were held together in the middle with duct tape.

Angel extended him the same monotone courtesy as all our customers. "Yes?" she asked.

"I'm Oscar Tenfor and I'd like to take flying lessons."

The law at Derry Air, as laid down by owner Irving Mingy and applied by Angel, was that on-the-spot flights were to be conducted whenever a pilot was available. The receptionist called Larry over and introduced him to the new customer.

I was flying with a student in the circuit at the time. I saw the familiar stationwagon in our parking lot.

"Derry Tower, Tango Victor Hotel downwind Runway 24 touch and go with an Elmer alert."

Larry heard me on the office radio and started to put two and two together.

"Whatcha got in the box there, Oscar?" Larry asked.

"A radio monitor," Oscar replied. "I want to take flying lessons so I can hear the pilots making mistakes on the frequencies."

Chapter Twenty-five

Very extinguished

Raffi was excited. Raffi Dharawala was always excited. He was a hyperactive student pilot who charged headfirst through life, excited and happy. I liked Raffi but he was almost impossible to teach. His emotions and actions worked too far ahead of his brain.

Raffi had emigrated to Derry from the Far East to work as a chemist. He had come to Derry Air to realize a dream of learning to fly. I was his instructor. After a few lessons it was easy for me to imagine Raffi charging around a chemical lab knocking over important experiments. The unique stains and holes in his clothes were a testament to this being a regular occurrence. I considered that maybe the chemical company had hired Raffi because he was expected to accidentally discover the next super substance.

"I am so happy to be making another lesson for de birds," he said with a huge grin.

I was briefing Raffi on the introduction to takeoffs, the circuit and landings.

"You mean a flying lesson," I corrected.

"Yes, yes, making like bird make me very happy."

The briefing wasn't going well. Raffi was too excited to listen.

"Well, Raffi, let's forget the briefing and make like the birds. I'll demonstrate the takeoffs and landings in the airplane."

He scrambled out of his seat. "Oh, yes. Dis will be terribly exciting."

"I hope not."

I signed us out at the flight desk, picked up the aircraft logbook and herded Raffi toward the door.

The builders of the Derry Air office had not been kind to Raffi. They had made the inner door open in. The hinges were on the left. The outer

147

door swung out and was hung on right-hand hinges. This complexity was compounded by being backwards to the way they worked when Raffi had come into the building. This guaranteed that the hyperactive chemist would struggle with one or both doors trying to get out.

"Push, Raffi," I offered when he reached the second door. "No, push on the left side."

"Excuse me," he said, smiling apologetically, "everyt'ing in dis country works opposite."

"We do that on purpose," I agreed. "It creates a huge market for instructors. We are flying Tango Victor Hotel today," I said, pointing at one of the flying school Cherokees. Raffi eagerly headed to the Piper.

I reviewed the walkaround with him. When we were done, he hopped on the right wingwalk, opened the door and dropped into the right seat. Raffi had long legs so he reached under the left seat to roll it back. He reached too far. He grabbed the fire extinguisher instead of the seat bar and squeezed it. I was standing on the ground behind the wing. There was a "whoosh" and the cockpit immediately filled with fine white powder. I couldn't see anything inside the airplane but I could hear Raffi coughing and sputtering. I jumped onto the wing, reached in and grabbed him.

"Come on, Raffi. It's the fire extinguisher. Climb out this way."

I pulled on his shirt. Raffi struggled out of the cockpit onto the wing. He was covered with dry extinguisher powder. He looked like a gingerbread man doused with icing sugar.

I brushed off his face the best I could with my hand. "Come on. We'll get you cleaned up."

"Excuse me," he spit the words out with more powder, "where is de fire?"

I helped him off the wing. "No fire, Raffi. You just discharged the fire extinguisher when you reached under the seat."

"I did dat?"

I led him around the aircraft. "Yes, you must have pulled the wrong handle when you were trying to adjust the seat. Come this way."

"Oh my. Dis is very disappointing," he said trying to brush off the chemical. A white cloud followed us as we crossed the ramp.

"Don't worry about it. We'll get you cleaned up and find another airplane."

I steered him to the maintenance hangar. Chief mechanic Darcy Philips spotted us from across the shop. "Whoa! Here come the chemicalmen. Where's the fire?"

"No fire, Darcy," I replied. "Just an accidental discharge. Where's the vacuum?"

"Bring him over here."

I helped Raffi negotiate his way between the airplanes to the back of

the shop. He talked the whole way.

"I am exceeding sorry about dis. It is exceptionally inconvenient of myself."

He occasionally wiped his mouth trying to get rid of the powder.

"It's okay, Raffi," I offered. "Maybe this will encourage you to invent a better tasting powder for fire extinguishers."

Darcy plugged in the shop vacuum and ran the nozzle up and down while the chemist danced around spouting apologies.

"Hold still a minute while I do your hair," Darcy said.

The vacuum removed the worst of the fine powder which went right through the filter and formed a cloud in the back of the shop.

Darcy looked at me. "That should do it. You can clean the shop when you're done flying."

I led Raffi into the office to see if another Cherokee was available. We were in luck. Raffi and I headed back out to the ramp.

We did a quick walkaround inspection together. When Raffi climbed onto the wing, I said, "Look under the left seat and you'll see the fire extinguisher. While you're looking, check the pressure gauge on it to see if it's charged up, but don't pull the handle."

Raffi stuck his head down in front of the seat. When he came up again, he said, "I'm very sorry but dis gauge reads 'zero'."

"Climb out and let me have a look."

"I didn't touch it," Raffi said, hopping off the wing.

"It's okay. It's not your fault."

I climbed onto the wing and leaned into the cockpit headfirst. Raffi was right. The indicator needle on the extinguisher was hard on zero. I released the clamp and removed the bottle from its bracket.

"I'll get us another one, Raffi," I said. You climb in but don't start anything until I get back."

I hotfooted to the shop. Darcy saw me coming. "Well here comes powder-man again. There's no fire in here either."

"Thanks, smart mouth. Do you have another fire extinguisher?"

"What's wrong with that one?"

"It's dead," I said. I pointed it at him and squeezed the trigger. "See?"

I was only half right. The gauge was dead but the contents were very much alive. Darcy was about fifteen feet away. A powerful stream of white powder exploded across the shop and nailed the little mechanic square in the chest. I released the lever immediately but not before Darcy disappeared in a cloud of profanity.

Huey, Duey and Louey walked into the shop in single file at that moment. They had been summoned to clean the inside of the other aircraft.

"Hey, cool," Huey said to me. "Can I try that?"

Duey spoke in a mock John Wayne voice, "My name's Darcy, but folks call me Dusty."

"Oh Frosty!" Louey exclaimed. "Don't let the children hear you saying those bad words."

Chapter Twenty-six

Reincarnated

"Marathon" Melville had completed 160 hours of flying lessons, six runs through ground school and three practice flight tests. His knowledge of the systems on the Derry Air Cherokee 140s was the best of any flying school customer. The round little farm boy flew the airplanes better than most student pilots. He had even passed the written exam (63 per cent on only his third try).

I decided that Melville Passmore was ready to become a Private Pilot. But that decision was not mine to make. Melville still had to pass a flight test.

Eric was a government designated flight test examiner. I was confident that Melville would fly a good test with him. My only problem was that the government had to be notified of all flight tests. The inspectors at the Flight Standards Regional Headquarters had the option of conducting tests as a spot check on the industry. If they decided to fly with Melville, chances were good that he would fail.

The trouble was how Melville reacted to authority. If an instructor asked Melville to fly low down the street of a town to read the name on the post office as a method of navigation, he would do it. I know because Larry asked Melville to do that on one of his pre-flight tests. Larry was treated to a low level flying demonstration along the main street of Norwich.

I sat in on Larry's de-briefing. "He did a great job," Larry laughed. "He missed all the trees, stayed over the wires and hit the stop light on a green."

Melville looked at the floor and scuffed his boots while Larry related the episode.

"He even managed to read the sign on the post office as we went by but it didn't do him any good."

"Why is that?" I asked.

"Tell him, Melville." Larry chuckled.

Without looking up, Melville mumbled, "The sign said, 'Postes Canada Post'."

I gave Melville more lessons. Another instructor flew with Melville on another practice test without throwing him any curves. I booked Melville with Eric for the next week. Angel mailed the notification to the government and I crossed my toes hoping that miserable old Inspector Kennedy would not show up on the appointed day. If he saw my name under "recommending instructor," there was a good chance he might.

The day came and the government didn't. Eric flew the test. The results of the flight were written all over Melville's face as he charged into the Derry Air lounge from the ramp.

"I passed! I passed!"

I grabbed his hand and slapped him on the back. "Way to go Captain Passmore!" He was jumping up and down with excitement. It was like shaking hands with a jackhammer.

Melville ran around the office, the shop and the linecrew shack telling everyone that he had passed. Eric and I waited for him to settle down so we could go over his performance.

"You know, he's not going to hear a word you say," I offered.

"Yah, I know," Eric grinned, "but he did a good job."

When we got Melville to sit down, the chief instructor listed several exercises that had been scored low but emphasized that overall Melville had flown well and deserved to be a licenced pilot. A customer walked into the office. Melville jumped up and ran over to tell him his news.

I pointed to the items with the low marks. "He flew those without any trouble before," I moaned.

"I'm sure," Eric replied, "but he was nervous. These scores measure his performance on a test, not his ability as a pilot. Don't worry about it. Assign him some solo practice and turn him loose."

"Okay."

That's what I did. Melville flew some practice and Angel sent in his pilot licence application.

A couple of days later, I received a phone call from Inspector Kennedy. The tone of his voice was stone-cold miserable.

"I was just reviewing a flight test report on a student pilot that you recommended," he barked sternly.

"Yes sir?" I said as politely as possible. "And a fine young pilot he is." I had no idea what he wanted. I had been instructing for three years and the government had never called me about flight test results.

"His scores are low," he continued.

"Yes, some of them are," I replied carefully. "They have been reviewed with the customer," I added hopefully. "Some solo practice was assigned."

My mind raced. I didn't know if Kennedy could reverse Melville's pass.

The inspector took a long breath on the phone. "How confident are you in this student's abilities as a Private Pilot?"

I had never heard of a student being asked to re-fly a passed test. I got brave.

"If I didn't think Mr. Passmore's flying abilities were above standard, I would not have recommended him for the test," I said. I tried to sound confident.

This was greeted with another pause. "Tell me," Kennedy finally said, "would you send your family flying with Mr. Passmore?"

It was a strange question. It ticked me off. I decided that Kennedy couldn't do anything unless I conceded some doubt regarding the little farmer's flying. Then I'd have to agree to a retest with a government inspector.

"Well sir, I would if I could, but my wife and children were killed in a plane crash."

It was a lie. My wife was alive and hoping that I'd get home before her to feed the horses. We had no children.

"I'm sorry to hear that," he said flatly. But he didn't give up. "This student's hours are high and his scores are low."

"Don't worry, sir. He's a good pilot; a credit to the system."

"I just wanted to make sure of his ability," Kennedy continued.

"Thanks for calling," I replied.

"Right." He hung up.

I heard nothing further. A couple of weeks later, Melville came into the flying school proudly waving the permanent pilot licence that he had received in the mail.

Some time after that, Inspector Kennedy came to Derry Air and conducted a routine renewal flight test on one of the other instructors. I spoke to him briefly but nothing was said about the phone call over Melville's marks.

That same day I had arranged with my wife Susan to pick me up at the airport later in the afternoon. Kennedy was leaving as she came in.

"Inspector Kennedy, I'd like you to meet my wife Susan. Inspector Kennedy does flight tests for the government," I explained.

Susan was in ladies retail clothing sales. She liked to meet people. "Pleased to meet you," she said, offering Kennedy a handshake.

The stone-faced inspector stopped and shook her hand. "Likewise," he said almost pleasantly. "Yes, I have flown with your husband in the past," he added. The small talk was out of character.

"Me too," Susan offered with a smile, "although he probably behaves himself better flying with you."

I was wishing I hadn't bothered to introduce them.

Kennedy continued the conversation. "You two both look 'lively'. You must have been married recently. My congratulations."

What has come over this man? I asked myself.

"Oh, thank you," Susan gushed. "I'm glad we still look fresh together but we've been married for years."

"But you must be his second wife," Kennedy continued.

Then it hit me.

"Yes, she is," I blurted out. I grabbed Susan and shoved her toward the door, "and we have to get going. Bye now."

I hustled my protesting wife outside.

"What was that all about?" Susan boomed, shrugging off my grip.

"I'll explain later," I said quickly.

"You'll explain sooner than later and it better be good."

Chapter Twenty-seven

Belly flop

Larry landed the Twin Comanche on the runway with the wheels retracted. In hindsight, the accident was predictable. Larry was practising circuits with a student. The lesson was an introduction to takeoffs and landings on the multi-engine course.

The customer was a "hummer." He hummed when he was nervous. There was plenty to start him buzzing during his first circuits in the Twin Comanche. The airplane had twice the power and three times the systems as the Piper Cherokees that Derry Air used for basic training. The student had to contend with propeller adjustments, manifold pressure and landing gear retraction while blasting around the patch at 50 per cent more speed than in a Cherokee.

"He hummed as soon as we got into the airplane," Larry told us later. "It was like a radio station broadcasting slightly off frequency. When we took off, the hum elevated to a squeal like bad brakes on an old truck. It was very annoying."

Larry and Hummer were sharing the circuit with a student from the neighbouring flying school. He was practising takeoffs and landings in a Cessna 150. The solo student was headed for trouble. He had discovered that if he left some power on during the landing it bought him more time over the runway to set up the touchdown. On each successive approach he left the throttle in a little further. Runway 24 was 6,000 feet long so there was no problem with distance but when he tried to land with the engine at 1,500 rpm, he touched down nosewheel first. The airplane rebounded back into the air. The student pushed forward. The nose dropped and the airplane kangarooed off it's front tire again, harder this time. This set up a series of nose up and down oscillations that the student made worse by reacting half a beat behind the airplane. Nose bounce number three was harder, number four harder still. If the student had done an overshoot at

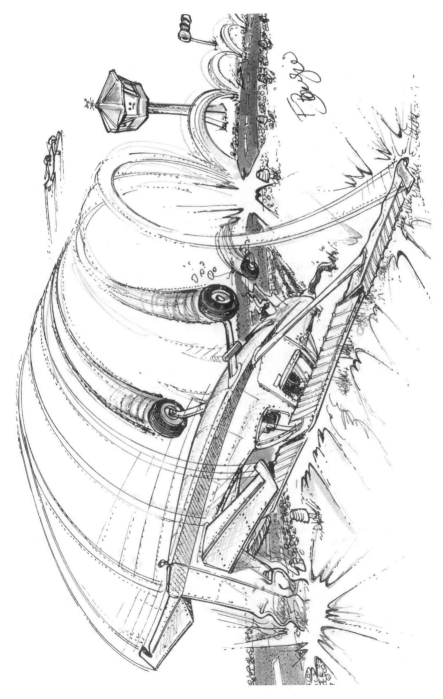

157

that point he would have been all right but he didn't. On the fifth bounce, the nosewheel sheared off and the propeller dug into the asphalt. The prop stopped but the internal parts in the engine kept going. In one second the engine was destroyed. The Cessna skidded to the side of the runway where it dug into the grass and flipped onto its back.

Larry happened to see the accident from the downwind leg of the circuit.

"Alpha India Romeo, extend your downwind," the tower controller said. "We have a problem on the runway."

"Derry Tower, India Romeo. I check. Let me land. I've got a fire extinguisher. I can help."

Larry took control from his student. He chopped the power on both engines and started a turn toward the runway.

"India Romeo, roger. Land Runway 24 at your own discretion. Check the aircraft off to the side. Wind two five zero at twelve. Check gear down."

"India Romeo," Larry replied.

His student spotted the wreck on the edge of the runway. He hummed louder. Larry tipped the airplane on its side for a tight circuit to a landing. Hummer went into overdrive.

"It sounded like a high-speed freight train with all its wheels locked," Larry said.

He dove for the runway intent on getting to the wreck as soon as possible. He kept his speed up until the flare-out, then he closed the throttles. The hum grew to a squealing crescendo as the "gear up" horn joined the chorus. Larry ignored it and concentrated on the landing. He didn't even hear the propeller tips hitting the asphalt. The airplane flopped on its belly and skidded to a stop beside the inverted Cessna.

Despite the shock of what he had just done or because of it, Larry didn't lose sight of his mission. He grabbed the fire extinguisher from under the pilot's seat, leaped out of the airplane and ran to the wreck where he rescued the student pilot who was hanging upside down in the Cessna. There were two injuries among the three pilots involved. The solo student cracked his head and Larry twisted his ankle.

When he returned from the hospital with his foot bound up and walking with crutches he held court with the other instructors during a coffee break.

"I learned three things today: One, don't allow humming in your airplane; two, when you land wheels up, you don't leap off the back of the wing because you are already on the ground; and third, when you release the seat belt of someone hanging upside down in an airplane, they fall on their head."

Chapter Twenty-eight

We're here to help you

Derry Air chief mechanic Darcy Philips ran a tight shop. He had a reputation for turning out good work at fair prices. The testament to this was the steady stream of customers bringing aircraft to Derry Air for inspections and repairs.

Apparently Darcy's sterling reputation was not known to everyone. Shortly after Derry Air instructor Larry Buttons landed the Twin Comanche on its belly, someone in the government headquarters sent a team of senior airworthiness inspectors to blitz our shop. It seemed unnecessary. The accident was caused by pilot brain fade, not faulty maintenance.

At ten o'clock on a Monday morning, three trench coats walked into the shop carrying clipboards. Darcy's dog Pilot barked a warning as soon as they opened the pedestrian door into the hangar. Darcy knew all the local inspectors but these were strangers. He squirted out of his office immediately.

"Hi, there. Can I help you?"

The three men introduced themselves. Darcy shook their hands and ushered them into his office.

Later in the morning, he came into the flight lounge during an instructor coffee break and told us about the visit.

"They reminded me of Curly, Harry and Moe," Darcy said with a smile. "They told me that they were on a maintenance base inspection. They wanted to check the aircraft in the shop, our record keeping, our spare parts tracing system and the quarantine stores."

"Sounds pretty serious," I said.

"Oh, these guys are serious. Curly is a top gun from Ottawa. Harry and Moe are senior inspectors pulled from other regions for this swoop."

"Wow. How did you get rid of them?" Eric asked.

"I didn't. They're in the shop now."

"How can you sit here and calmly drink coffee while they're in there ripping around?"

"Easy. They're doing my job. I'm the one who checks the aircraft maintenance; I monitor the record keeping and I trace the spare parts. They're in there working for me so I'm in here drinking coffee with you."

"Aren't you worried about what they'll find?" Henry asked.

"No. Finding things is why we do inspections. Before they came, Leonard had pulled Tango Victor Hotel into the shop for a 100-hour. He had just dropped the panels on it. I told Curly we had completed the inspection and were about to button it up. I invited them to inspect it before we were done. Harry and Moe are doing that right now. Curly is on the Microfische reader checking the list of Airworthiness Directives for Cherokees. They are doing the inspection. I love having the government do my work."

Henry continued to press the nonchalant engineer. "But are they going to find snags?"

"If there are snags, they'd better find them. These guys are supposed to be the best. In the meantime, I have Leonard working on something else. We're saving all kinds of money. When they're done, I'll get Leonard to fix the discrepancies on their list."

"But they could shut you down," Eric suggested.

Darcy waved the comment off with his hand as he took a gulp of coffee. "Naw. If I'm out of business then they're out of business. These guys are inspectors. Their job is find and report snags. Right now they're happy as pigs because TVH hasn't seen maintenance for a month. If I had known in advance that they were coming we could have thrown a few duff parts on her and made them even happier."

It sounded to me like Darcy was being too cocky but he had been in business for a long time.

"I'd think the more they find wrong, the more they'll look," I said. "They could be here for a week."

"I hope they're here two weeks," Darcy exclaimed. "They could inspect the whole fleet."

I was working the late shift that day. I was scheduled to fly Tango Victor Hotel that evening with three different students starting at six o'clock. The shop normally has 100-hour inspections done in one day. There were no other aircraft available on the booking sheets. I mentioned this to Darcy when I saw him again that afternoon.

"Did you get a snag list from Curly, Harry and Moe yet?" I asked.

"No, they might be good but they're not fast. It'll be a while."

I showed him the booking sheet. "Shall I cancel my students?"

"No, no; bite your tongue. We don't cancel lessons at Derry Air. The airplane will be ready."

"You won't have time to fix snags and put the aircraft together today."

"You worry too much," Darcy said. "Curly and his gang won't finish their inspection until tomorrow. They have to leave before four o'clock so they can drive to their hotel on government time. Since they haven't confronted me with a snag list, there are no reported snags on the airplane. It only has 96 hours on it since the last 100-hour so we can still fly it four hours." Darcy was smiling the whole time he was talking. "Leonard and I will have the airplane buttoned up and ready to go for you by six. We'll chalk the wheel locations on the floor and put it back in the same spot with the panels off by the time the three musketeers come back at 09:30 tomorrow."

I shook my head. "You're playing with fire."

"Don't worry about it. It's all legal but you can do me a favour."

"What's that?"

"Don't wreck the airplane."

The Cherokee was out of the hangar and ready to go by six o'clock. I flew it all evening. I helped lineman Crazy Jim close up that night. We pushed Tango Victor Hotel back into the shop and parked it on the chalk marks.

The next day I was on the late shift again. When I arrived before noon, I walked into the shop before going to the lounge. I was curious to see what was happening. Cherokee Tango Victor Hotel was not there. There were no inspectors in sight. Darcy was sitting in his office.

"Where are your three assistants?" I asked.

He looked up and smiled. "Not here," he said. "They left when their office called. Somebody got it wrong. They were supposed to be blitzing Dawn Air."

Chapter Twenty-nine

Goin' to Derry

Melville Passmore was in love. The Derry Air customer had met a girl who was new to his church group.

"She might be sweet on me," he said to me one day at the flying school. "I wanna take her on a flyin' date. Maybe somewhere nice for dinner."

"Dinner" to the round farmer was at noon. I opened a map of the area. I knew he had a limited budget so I didn't look far.

"On a Saturday you can get dinner at Brantford or London to the west."

"Brantford is not very far," he replied, "and there's a control tower in London."

Melville was nervous about talking on the radio.

"Okay, go northwest to Hanover or north to Brampton."

"Are they busy?"

"Yes."

His face said I should keep looking.

"Well how about Lindsay? You could loop around the top of Toronto and stay under the terminal airspace," I suggested. I traced my finger on the map to the little airport northeast of Toronto. "It's an hour away but it isn't too busy and there's a highway restaurant right on the field."

"Good," he said. "I'll book Lindsay for next weekend."

"Okay, Tiger. Go for it."

Melville's nickname at Derry Air was "Marathon." He had taken a long time to finish his pilot licence. He flew well when left to figure things out for himself but he had difficulty adapting his country way of learning to the government way of teaching. During his training he had been a round peg trying to fit into a square hole. I knew because I had been his instructor. His upcoming "date" would be his first flight with a

passenger.

The appointed day came. I arranged to be on the ground when Melville arrived with his girlfriend. His face was beaming when he introduced us.

"This is Faith," he said proudly.

"Pleased to meet you," I said.

"Thank you," she replied in a quiet voice. "Melville talks about you all the time."

"Only good things, I hope."

In his best farmer style, Melville licked his lips, hauled in his tongue, looked both ways, "Betcha never thought I'd show you a girl like this!"

The statement was bold but genuine. Faith blushed.

Melville was right. I had expected the chubby, grubby farm boy to arrive with a chubby, grubby farm girl. Faith was short like Melville but otherwise the opposite. Her face was scrubbed and her curly hair shone. She was wearing a clean red car coat over a pretty hand-knit sweater and a pleated skirt. Her dress was a contrast to Melville's coveralls. So was her calm manner and light perfume.

"Melville, you're a lucky man to be escorting such a lovely girl," I replied.

He puffed his chest out and grinned. Then he handed me his map. "I marked the route, checked the weather and filed a flight plan, just like you taught me," he said, "but you look at it, like you always do."

"I'd be glad to Melville."

His route and his flight plan looked good. I didn't tell him, but I had also called flight service and asked for the weather to Lindsay. The forecast was a great day for winter flying. A high pressure system was moving in bringing sunny skies and cool temperatures.

"Everything is fine, Melville," I said and then added some last minute advice. "When you fly around Toronto, listen on the terminal frequency for other traffic in your area. And take the engine intake plugs with you. Use them in Lindsay to keep the oil warm while you're having dinner."

"Okay," he replied. He was excited. He took the girl's hand. "Let's go, Faith."

"Don't forget to sign out with Angel," I called after him.

"Oh, yah."

He towed the girl over to the flight desk. "Angel, this is Faith. Betcha never thought I'd show you a girl like this!"

I flew with seveal students around Derry in clear skies. I didn't know that a rare southeast wind had developed over Lake Ontario and pushed extra moisture over Toronto. Snow showers blanketed the area unexpectedly.

When I returned from one of the lessons, Angel told me to call the

Derry Control Tower.

I picked up the direct line.

"Tower here."

"You called me?"

"Yes. Thought you'd like to know that Melville declared an emergency over downtown Toronto. Apparently it's snowing over there. He's still airborne but they don't know for how long."

It was news that any flying instructor would dread.

"What's his emergency?" I asked.

"I don't know. I guess it's below VFR. They called us because they're tracking him on radar and he's headed this way. I'll call back as soon as I hear more."

"Thanks."

I was worried beyond belief but I didn't know what to be worried about. Melville could fly in reduced visibility. The situation would have to be serious for him to use the radio and to declare an emrgency.

As the unanswered questions flooded my head, the tower line rang. I grabbed it.

"Yes?"

"Melville's okay. He flew out of the snow and is approaching the Derry Control Zone."

"Wow. Thank you. So what was the emergency all about?"

"I don't know."

"Okay. Thanks again."

Before I went flying with my next customer, I asked Angel to have Melville wait for me to return.

While my student and I were taking off, Melville joined the circuit and landed. He was shouting on the radio but that was normal. When I returned, Melville and his girlfriend were in the lounge.

The farmer hovered nervously behind me while I finished with my student. When I was done, I turned in his direction. He was watching the floor as he shifted his weight from one foot to the other.

"So, Ace," I said, "I heard you had a little problem."

He took a big breath, licked his lips, looked both ways and pulled in his tongue. "Well, the controller in Toronto told me to go a different way. I'm glad you showed me instrument flying."

"The weather was bad?"

"Yah. On the way back, it started snowin' a little." The round farmer took another breath, licked his lips and continued. "I listened to Toronto Terminal like you said. I heard him callin', 'Westbound aircraft north of Toronto, say your altitude.' He called twice so I picked up the microphone and said I was at 2,000 feet."

Melville spoke with a worried edge to his voice. It warned of worse to come. I listened.

"He wanted to know all kinds of stuff: my aircraft type, registration, where I was goin'. He asked if I was instrument rated."

"What did you say?"

"I told him I was in Cherokee Tango Victor Hotel and I was goin' to Derry. I said the airplane had instruments and I was usin' them. Then he asked my flight conditions. I said it was smooth and it was snowin' a bit."

Melville had done well during the instrument flying lessons on the Private Pilot Course. It was something that he could figure out for himself. I could picture him flying along in light snow with his tongue hanging out while he concentrated on the map, the ground and the instruments. I imagined that he thought it was okay to be there because the flight service specialist had told him the weather was going to be fine.

"Then he asked me if I was declarin' an emergency."

"What did you say?"

"I said no, I was goin' to Derry."

I smiled to myself. "What did he say to that?"

Melville licked his lips and hauled in his tongue. Faith stood calmly beside him. "He said the terminal area was below VFR and I should stay away."

"What did you do?"

Melville frowned. "He sounded cross. I didn't want to do anythin' wrong so I thought I should turn around and stay out of his area by goin' to the east."

"Good."

"No, not good. He told me to call Buttonville Tower. When I did, the guy said they were below VFR and asked my intentions. I said I was goin' to Derry. Then he wanted to know if I was declarin' an emergency. I said no, I was goin' to Derry. He said I should stay clear of the zone, so I did. Those guys sure know how to confuse a fella."

"When did you declare an emergency?"

"Not 'til later. When I passed Buttonville, I turned south. The controller told me to call Oshawa Tower."

"Did you?"

"Yah. That guy gave me the weather. It was worse. He said, 'Say your intentions.' I said that I was goin' to Derry. Then he asked if I was declarin' an emergency. I told him I was goin' to Derry. He said I would have to remain clear of their control zone."

There was room between Toronto's Terminal Area and Oshawa's Control Zone to fly south without entering either airspace. Melville must have been busy. He would have been hand-flying all the way.

"Did you use the VOR?

"Yah, the map and the VOR. There wasn't much time for sightseeing but then there wasn't much to see."

"What altitude were you at?"

"Two thousand."

"What did you do then?"

"The guy in the tower at Oshawa told me to switch to Toronto Termi-nal. I didn't want to but I did. It was the same guy as before. He asked me if I was declarin' an emergency. I said no, I was goin' to Derry. He said to stay below 1,700 feet to remain clear of the terminal area. I descended to 1,500."

The little farmer looked at me sideways to see my reaction. "It's hard doin' all that flyin' and talkin'," he said.

"I know."

Melville would then be flying along the shoreline at 1,500 feet and heading toward downtown Toronto .

"How did you get past Toronto?"

Melville licked his lips nervously and pulled his tongue back in. "The terminal guy told me to call Toronto Island Tower. The first thing he said was, 'Are you declarin' an emergency?' I said, 'No I'm goin' to Derry.' He told me to remain clear of the control zone."

With that, Melville stopped talking. I waited. He looked at the floor. He obviously didn't want to tell me what had happened next.

The only way around the Toronto Island airspace was to fly south, five miles over Lake Ontario.

"What did you do?" I asked quietly.

No reply.

"What did you say to him, Melville?"

"I told him that I couldn't swim so I didn't want to fly around. He told me that their weather was 500 feet obscured and a half a mile in snow. He said to enter the zone I would have to declare an emergency."

Melville went quiet again.

"It's okay, Melville. I'm not going to do anything. Just tell me what happened."

He spoke very softly. "That's when I declared an emergency."

"Okay. Then what."

"At first he told me to stand by but then he cleared me to land on any runway, gave me the wind and advised me to stay south of the shoreline until I had the field in sight."

The Toronto Island Airport was next to the downtown core. The tallest building, the CN Tower, at one time the tallest freestanding structure in the world, was less than a kilometre away.

"Good advice," I said.

"No, not good. I told him I didn't wanna land. I was goin' to Derry."

"How happy was he about that?"

Melville looked at me sideways. His tongue was at full hang.

"He didn't say nothin' for awhile. Then he told me that pilots declare emergencies in bad weather so they can land. I said I'd rather fly in snow than try to land in it."

It was bold talk for the shy farmer. I couldn't help smiling.

"What did he say?" I asked.

"He told me the weather was VFR in Derry."

"What did you say to that?"

"Nothin'. I just kept flyin' and hopin' he didn't have any other ideas. He asked me to call clear of his control zone, so I did. Then he told me to advise him of any altitude changes. Those guys sure can make it hard even when there isn't any other traffic. I was having trouble just flyin'."

"They were trying to help in their own way, Melville," I said.

"Am I in trouble now?" the little farmer asked.

"I don't know," I said honestly. "The important thing is that you applied your own judgement and skill to fly out of a bad situation."

He watched his feet scuff at the floor.

"Next time, you could turn around as soon as you see the snow. You could have flown back to Lindsay and waited for better weather."

Melville looked up. "Oh no," he said, shaking his head. "I'd 'ave been in worse trouble."

"How do you figure that?"

Melville scratched his head and gave Faith a funny look. "Faith's dad said if I don't have her back home by supper time, he'd whup me good." He looked at his watch. "We gotta run."

Chapter Thirty

Copilot

Darcy came into the Derry Air flight lounge with his dog following him. I was finishing a post-flight briefing with a student.

"Pilot and I are going to test fly a Cherokee 140," Darcy said. "Wanna come?"

"Sure," I said, checking my watch. "I've got 30 minutes."

"Lots of time," he replied. He signed us out.

I followed the pair outside. When we reached the airplane, Darcy motioned for me to get in first. "I've already checked it over," he said.

I climbed onto the right wing and slid over to the left front seat. Pilot hopped onto the wingwalk behind me. Darcy climbed up and held the seat forward so the dog could jump into the back. The mechanic sat down in the right seat and rotated his finger in the air to signal a start-up.

"We'll do a local flight to the southwest," he said. "I changed the carburetor heat box and I want to test it in the air."

I started the engine, called the control tower and taxied out to the active runway. Pilot moved constantly back and forth across the rear seats to see out the windows on either side. I completed a run-up check and received a take-off clearance. As soon as I pulled onto the runway, Pilot sat down between the back seats and stared straight ahead between Darcy and me. We lifted off and climbed toward the practice area. Darcy applied the carburetor heat a couple of times. It worked fine. I levelled off and throttled back. He tried it again. No problem.

"Okay," he said, "give me a medium turn."

"The carb heat is going to work differently in a turn?" I asked.

"I didn't say it would," Darcy replied.

I should have known better than to question the chief engineer. It never did any good.

"Which way?"

"Your choice."

I banked left. The dog sat still in the back. I looked at Darcy.

"Now increase the bank."

As soon as I rolled past 30 degrees, Pilot started to bark. It was the same constant series of sharp barks that she used when she needed help with a box over a hose on the shop floor. I looked at Darcy again.

"Now less bank," he said.

I applied opposite aileron. As the bank decreased, the barking stopped.

171

I rolled back into a steep turn. Pilot started barking again and didn't stop until I reduced the angle of the turn.

"That's neat," I said. "She's a built-in copilot."

"Try slow flight," Darcy said.

I slowed the airplane down. I could see Pilot sitting quietly out of the corner of my eye. As the speed dropped below 85 mph, the dog did nothing. At 70 mph, she started to bark. I smiled at Darcy.

"Go ahead and stall it," he said.

At 65 mph, the stall horn sounded. Pilot barked louder. I continued to raise the nose of the aircraft higher. As we approached the stall, Pilot was on her feet and leaning forward to bark in my ear. When the airplane started the pre-stall buffet, the barking switched to a loud growl as the little dog grabbed my right sleeve with her mouth and shook it. She continued this as the nose dropped and I initiated a stall recovery. As soon as the airplane regained flying speed, she let go and sat down quietly.

"That's pretty clever," I said. "What else can she do?"

"Put your hand on my knee."

"No thanks," I said.

Darcy grinned.

We headed back to the airport. Throughout the approach and landing, Pilot sat quietly but attentively between the back seats.

"How come she didn't bark when I slowed down that time?"

"I said she was dumb but even a pilot knows when you're landing."

Pilot became the topic of conversation with the instructors around the coffee maker. We speculated whether the government would count student flights as solo if Pilot went along as a copilot. The flights would be safer with the little dog sitting next to the student, barking whenever the airspeed got too low or the bank too steep.

The next time Darcy joined us for coffee, we asked him about the idea.

"Naw," he replied. "We need her in the shop."

"You probably have her doing inspections and changing engines when we're not looking," Chief Instructor Eric Daedalus suggested with a laugh.

"No, but I was going to train her to do the paperwork," Darcy said, "except the Department of Transport would never accept a signature from someone named 'Pilot'."

Chapter Thirty-one

Airplane roulette

There was extra money to be made at Derry Air in the spring. This was frost flying time. The nearby Niagara fruit farmers had a problem if there was a cold snap early in the growing season. Once the tender buds had started on the grape vines and fruit trees, they could be damaged by freezing. This was most likely to occur on calm, full moon nights in May.

There was a theoretical solution to the problem. If there was no wind, the temperature above the crop was warmer than on the ground. It was believed that an aircraft flying in the warm air could displace it downward and save the buds from freezing. The multi-million dollar fruit growing industry was willing to bet that it worked.

Derry Air owner Irving Mingy contracted with the Niagara Fruit Growers Association to provide aircraft in case of frost. The rate charged was triple the regular hourly cost of an airplane and pilot. There was a waiting list of farmers requesting the service. Eric asked me if I wanted to sign up for the extra duty.

I had seen aircraft crop spraying. It looked like fun. The pilot zipped across the field, pulled up at the end, flew a half lazy eight turnaround and buzzed the field again. It was legal low flying.

"Pilots receive triple the hourly pay," Eric offered.

I said, "Yes."

"There's one catch," he added. He was smiling. Eric always smiled but this one was a sneaky smile. "The next farm on the list is beside the farm Henry is flying. You'll have to coordinate your passes so you don't run into each other."

Henry Rains was a good pilot and a friend. "No problem," I replied.

"You're on. Plan to visit the field on the ground to meet the farmer and to map out the obstructions."

"Okay."

I told Henry that I had signed up to frost fly the farm next to his.

"Whoa baby. You could be my worst nightmare."

"It should be fun."

"Three hours of low level formation flying in the dark starting at five o'clock in the morning is not fun for long."

"Don't we just fly opposite direction turns or something to stay apart?" I asked.

"Well, we can and we will but there's a big difference between talking about it and making it work when you're half asleep."

Henry sat down with me and drew a diagram. The two fields were long and skinny and lay at 90 degrees to each other. They ended at a road intersection that had hydro wires running in both directions. "So we have to pull up to clear the wires as we cross flight paths," Henry explained. "For each run, we have to fly in front of each other twice."

"Can't we just stagger the start of our runs so we're at opposite ends of the fields when we're turning?"

"Yes, and we will, but the fields are not equal lengths so the separation won't last."

"We could maintain contact on the radio to keep track of each other."

"Yes, and we will, but it won't be as easy as it sounds. Trust me."

"Why don't you do both fields and I'll fly the next farmer on the list?"

"We tried that but these are neighbouring grape farmers competing in the same market. Asking them to divide the cost of the service was like throwing two tom cats in a sack and shaking it. You and I will have to work it out. You visit the field on the ground and then we'll practise."

"Okay."

Eric gave me the name and number of my farmer. I called him and drove out to the field. Gilbert Drinkwater was a middle-aged, new breed of farmer. It was obvious from his no-nonsense manner that grape growing was strictly business. He was quick to tell me that the vineyard was just one of many that he operated in the area.

"And don't be wasting time flying over the field across the road," he said sternly.

"Yes sir," I replied. "There will be another pilot covering that area."

It didn't take me long to map the obstacles. There were no buildings on the property. It was 50 acres of grapes growing beside a county road. The field ended where another road crossed. There were hydro wires on the two road sides and that was it.

Before our practice session, Henry explained how to frost fly. "The idea is maximum displacement of air, so we operate at low speed with full flaps and lots of power. We fly racetrack turns since it isn't necessary for us to fly tracks immediately next to each other like crop sprayers. We save a little time by not flying teardrop turns."

Henry and I flew to the fields in daylight in separate Cherokee 140s. I watched from above while he demonstrated the technique. Then it was my turn to join the performance. I slowed down, dropped the flaps and dove for my farmer's field. I timed my first pass to cross Henry's vineyard while he was at the other end. It was a piece of cake: fly low over the grapes, pull up in a climbing, then descending turn and zoom over the field again.

It was uncanny how quickly we came together. It took three passes both ways, about six minutes, before we ended up on collison courses. It was like the airplanes were two powerful magnets. We had agreed that I would speed up in these cases since my field was shorter. That put Henry, the experienced frost flyer, in the position of avoiding me and not the other way around.

"Conflict," Henry called on the radio.

I clicked the microphone button in acknowledgement and pushed the power to full. With the flaps extended and a maximum fuel load, the airplane didn't accelerate very well. When I pulled up at the end, Henry had to turn slightly to fly behind me. We both did our racetrack turns to the left so we could keep each other in sight. Henry's turn was tighter. "Conflict," he called. I added power. Henry slowed down.

We practised for half an hour. The low flying was fun but it seemed we spent more time avoiding each other than anything else.

Back at the airport, Henry made a suggestion. "If you add power before a conflict develops then there is no conflict."

"Why didn't I think of that?"

Henry rolled his eyes. "With any luck, it will be a warm spring."

"Come on, Henry. It was fun."

"You won't say that after the third early morning in a row."

In theory the frost flying fit conveniently into the split shifts that Derry Air's instructors worked. Our regular schedules were from eight to six or noon to ten. The coldest part of a spring day came at dawn which started at five o'clock. We were contracted to fly over the crops from first light until the sun warmed things up, usually by eight o'clock. Then we either worked the regular shift and went home to bed or went home to sleep in the morning until noon.

A week after our practice flight, the call came in for possible frost. We were officially on standby which meant frost or not, we had to be at the airport at four o'clock the next morning.

Henry and I were on the late shift. We flew with students until ten o'clock that evening. Then we helped the linecrew, Huey, Duey and Louey gas up the airplanes and push them into the hangar.

"Are you going to be able to get yourself to work for four a.m. or should I come and get you out of bed?" Henry asked with a smirk.

"No problem," I replied with more confidence than I felt.

"Okay. I'll see you soon, hotshot."

It was 11:30 before I climbed into bed. I set the radio alarm clock for three a.m. It seemed like I had just dozed off when the music blared to life. I crawled out of bed, washed and ate some cereal. A full moon lit the path out to the car but it didn't seem very cold. There was no frost on the car.

Ten pilots and one lineman in various stages of sleepy and grumpy gathered around the coffee pot at Derry Air.

"Hey, he made it," Henry joked. "But is he awake and can he fly?"

He poured me a coffee and handed it to me.

The temperature at the airport was four degrees Celcius. A call to one of the farmers confirmed that there was no frost in the fields. I drank the coffee, drove home, set the alarm for 10:30 and went back to bed. I couldn't sleep. I was still excited from the prospect of frost flying. Besides, it was the normal time when I got up in the morning and my brain was spiked with caffeine. I got out of bed, dressed again, did some chores around the house and went to work.

"Frost call for tomorrow," Eric announced too cheerfully later that afternoon. It was five o'clock and my working day was half over.

That night I didn't feel too tired when I went to bed. It was just before midnight. When the alarm went off at three a.m., I woke up in a stupor. I felt like I had been drugged. I dragged myself out of bed. Washing, dressing and eating some breakfast seemed like monumental tasks. I didn't really wake up until I opened the back door and was hit with a wall of cold air. I was wearing just a spring jacket. I had to scrape frost off the car's windshield. It took full heat in the old Volkswagen to ward off the chill on the way to work.

I arrived at the airport in the dark at four o'clock. Duey had the doors of the hangar open and was standing there with his hands in his pockets and his eyes closed. The airplanes were still inside.

"Wanna hand there, Duey?" I asked.

His eyes popped open. "Ah, ah, no," he said slowly. "Eric said to leave them in 'til the last minute to keep the frost off."

"Good thinking. Come on in, I'll buy us a coffee."

Everyone was in the lounge. Henry came over to me right away.

"This looks like the real thing," he said. "Are you awake?"

I was awake after the cold car ride but I said, "No," just to bug him.

"Here. Let me help you," he said, taking my arm.

He escorted me over to the coffee maker, poured thick black liquid into a cup and handed it to me. I turned and gave it to Duey.

"I don't feel nearly as bad when I look at you," Henry laughed. He poured another coffee. "Maybe we should tie the airplanes together. I'll tow you and we'll do the fields in formation."

"Smart guy," I replied.

"Drink the coffee and take one with you," Henry laughed. "The need to pee will keep you awake during the flight."

"Good idea," I replied.

"When we get there," he said more seriously, "I'll start first and find the bottom of the warm air."

"Fine," I said, taking a sip. The coffee was as bad as usual but it tasted good.

"Any time you don't feel comfortable doing this, then break it off."

"Don't worry about me, Henry," I yawned.

"I'm not," he replied. "I'm worried about me. We're sharing the same airspace."

"I'm fine. I'm fine."

Eric interrupted us to give everyone a pep talk about staying alert and flying safely. "We'll do our walkarounds in the hangar and then pull all the aircraft out at once. Okay, grab your log books and keys. Let's go."

The moon was setting in the west when we took off. There was a hint of light to the northeast but looking down it was pitch black. I followed the navigation lights on Henry's aircraft. I have no idea how he found the fields in the dark.

"I'll drop down. You stay up here," he radioed.

"Okay."

"The cold air starts at 50 feet," he called after one pass. "Do your first runs at 100 feet and work down from there."

"All right."

I could not make out my field below so I set up for a pass at right angles to the direction Henry was flying. I knew there were no obstacles at 100 feet but it was scary descending in the dark. It felt like going down a ladder into a dark snake pit in bare feet. Something was going to bite me.

I levelled off, flew what I thought was a low pass and then checked the altimeter. I was at 500 feet. I pulled up, turned and descended to 300 feet. This time I could make out the dim outline of the road beside the field. I was missing it altogether. I had just jogged over to line up with the road when a set of lights flashed below. The farmer was there in his pick-up truck. During the next turn-around, I looked down and keyed on the truck lights. Halfway around the turn, the flashers started to drift. I was experiencing vertigo. I hit full power, pulled back and riveted my eyes on the instruments. My heart skipped and then raced. I got the wings level and the altimeter started to climb. I sneaked a peak outside. The truck was no longer in sight.

"Everything all right?" Henry asked over the radio.

"Okay, now," I replied. "I got disoriented."

"Do a 180 and you'll see the truck flashers."

"Thanks."

"Be careful. Crashing and burning is an expensive way to warm up the grapes."

I clicked the microphone in reply.

By the time I had lined up with the field again, I could make out some of the features on the ground in the growing light. I worked my next pass down to 100 feet.

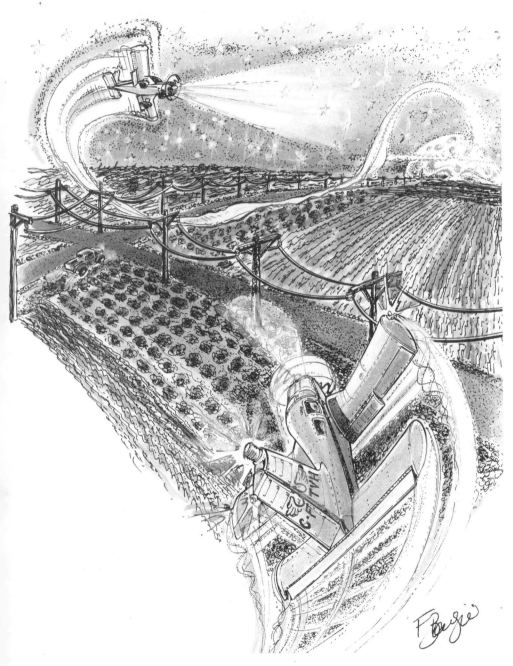

We flew for two hours. Henry was right. The fun and excitement of buzzing grapes wears off quickly. It became work. Every third or fourth pass, Henry called, "Conflict," and I would jockey my throttle. I was tired. The longer we flew, the worse I got at anticipating potential collisions. A couple of times Henry had to yell, "Conflict! Conflict!" to get my attention. Finally he called a halt. "I've got plus two degrees near the ground, let's break it off."

Back at Derry Air, he had not lost his sense of humour. "Go home, Rip van Winkle," he smiled, "and get some sleep. There's a good chance we'll be up for this tomorrow too."

I drove home. I was numb. I set the alarm for two hours later and passed out. When the radio came on, the smooth tones of the disc jockey blended into my dream. It didn't last. I was dreaming about frost flying. The realization that the radio didn't fit the dream woke me up.

I had a cold shower. It woke me up enough so I could drive to work. On the way I was thinking that this was not a smart way to make a living. At the airport I had to drag myself from lesson to lesson. My students got repeated practice and very little feedback that day.

Henry was the opposite. He was animated. When we saw each other between lessons, he was smiling and cheerful. "So Rip, sounds like we'll be on for frost again tomorrow. Maybe you'd better just sleep in the airplane tonight," he chuckled. "I'll start if for you in the morning and turn on the autopilot."

"Very funny."

Another time he was having coffee with Larry when I dragged myself in from a flight with a student. "Look, Larry," he announced, "here comes Sleepy, Dopey and Bashful all rolled into one." Later he came up to me and said, "Your eyes look like two pee holes in the snow. If I felt as bad as you look, I'd shoot myself." I don't know how he stayed so bouncy. He had to be as tired as I was. I didn't have the energy to respond to his jibes.

At five o'clock, Eric announced that we were on for frost in the morning. Henry continued his lighthearted quips until we had all the airplanes put away late that night. "I'd suggest we go out for a few beers," he laughed, "but I have to fly with you in six hours and I don't think you'd make it."

"Good night, Henry."

"Good night, Rip."

My wife poked me awake after the alarm woke her up. "Please don't volunteer for this next year," was all she said. She rolled over and went back to sleep. I almost joined her but managed to push myself out of bed just in time. The main thing that kept me going was the thought of the ribbing I'd take from Henry if I missed the flight.

There was frost. The flying was on. If Henry was tired, he didn't let it show.

"Hey, boys," he said when I arrived, "look what the cat dragged in. You need to open your eyes to find the plane."

"I'll be fine," I heard my voice say.

"Okay, let's go."

I flew but it wasn't pretty. My farmer had to flash his headlights to help me line up with the field in the early light. Twice I started to doze off during a run and forgot to turn. Each time Henry yelled at me over the radio. "Conflict! Conflict!" he barked. Our two aircraft were not on collision courses but he had seen me flying into the sunrise. His calls snapped me awake but I would be drowsy again soon. I don't know how he stayed awake enough to fly his airplane and mine too, but I was lucky he did.

My ordeal lasted two and a half hours before Henry finally called a halt. "I've got plus one degree," he radioed with a laugh. "If you've got one, that makes two. Let's split."

"Okay," I replied. I was so tired, my voice seemed to come from someone else.

I followed him back to the airport. I didn't really land the Cherokee. I just aimed it at the runway, chopped the power and drove it on. I parked the airplane and went straight to my car. The next thing I remember was waking up to the radio alarm. I rolled over. The time read "11:00." I couldn't recall the drive home or getting into bed.

I was still tired but I felt better after two hours of solid sleep. I went to work. Henry was having coffee with Eric when I walked into the lounge.

"Here comes the man who flies in his sleep," Henry chuckled.

"The good news," Eric announced, "is an approaching warm front. With any luck, we won't have to frost fly tomorrow morning."

"Shucks," Henry replied cheerfully. "I was looking forward to more extra pay."

"I'll take the extra sleep, thank you," I said as I poured myself a cup of coffee.

"I don't know what's the matter with today's youth," Henry said with a smirk. "They just can't take it."

With that, Henry's first student of the day walked in. "Time to go to work," he said hoisting himself out of the chair.

During that afternoon I dragged myself, zombie-like, from one lesson to another. Around four o'clock, I was conducting a ground briefing in the lounge. Henry was flying with a student. The office radio was on.

"Ah... Derry Tower... ah... this is Tango Victor Hotel?" The voice was from a nervous student.

"Tango Victor Hotel, Derry Tower, go ahead."

"Ah... I think my instructor passed out or something. I don't know what to do."

I had heard the call. I stopped teaching. I knew that Henry was in TVH. I recognized that Diana was the controller working the tower frequency. There was a pause before she answered.

"Tango Victor Hotel, are you flying straight and level?"

"Yes."

"Say your altitude."

"Three thousand."

"Are you able to hold that altitude straight and level?"

"Yes."

"Good. Does your instructor appear to be breathing?"

"Yes. He's snoring."

With that the student must have held the open microphone in front of Henry. An unmistakable vibrating snore was broadcast over the radio.

"Can you hear it?" the student asked.

"Yes. Try shaking him awake, Tango Victor Hotel, but continue to fly straight and level."

"I tried that but it didn't work," the student said. "Can I slap him?"

"Sure," Diana replied. "Give him a good slap in the face."

There was a long pause. Everyone in the Derry Air lounge had stopped what they were doing and was listening. I got up from the briefing cubicle, walked over to the flight desk and picked up the direct line to the control tower.

"Derry Tower," the other controller said over the telephone.

"It didn't help," the student was saying on the radio. His voice sounded a little desperate. "What do I do now?"

"The instructor in TVH is Henry Raines," I said to the off-air controller. "Tell Diana to yell into her microphone the phrase, 'Conflict, conflict, conflict!' That should wake him up."

"Ah... okay, I'll let her know."

"Trust me," I said. "The louder, the better. It has to do with frost flying. I can explain later."

"Stand by, Tango Victor Hotel," Diana was saying to the student pilot. There was another pause.

"Tango Victor Hotel, I'd like you to turn the volume up on your radio so it's really loud."

"Okay."

"Conflict, conflict, conflict!" Diana yelled.

A few seconds later, the student came back on the frequency. "It worked," he said. "He woke up and grabbed the control wheel."

There was the sound of Henry growling in the background.

"What the...?"

Chapter Thirty-two

What's next?

I was sitting by myself in the Derry Air lounge late one afternoon not long after the frost flying fiasco. Angel was at the flight desk filling in aircraft logbooks. I was waiting for a solo student to return from a flight.

I had been thinking a lot about my job lately. My progress at Derry Air had not been what I had planned. The instructing was worthwhile work but it seemed like I was always flying with misfit students. They were entertaining but did I want to spend the rest of my career with the likes of Marathon Melville, Edgar the Astronaut and Raffi the fire extinguisher king?

I had seen other instructors move on to the airline or corporate flying. They wore smart uniforms and flew the latest equipment. If they got up early in the morning it was not to chase warm air over grapes in the dark but to fly to some interesting destination. Since I had not been getting the multi-engine flights that would qualify me for a better job, maybe it was time for me to move on.

Darcy Philips came in with his dog. He was waiting for the airplane that my student was flying so he could drain the oil to start an inspection before going home. The Derry Air chief mechanic headed for the coffee maker. Pilot curled up on the floor.

"How long have you worked here, Darcy?" I asked.

"Twelve years of bliss," he said sarcastically. He poured himself a coffee. "Want some?" he asked, holding up the pot.

"No thanks."

He took a seat next to the dog. "Why do you ask?"

"I just wondered how come you haven't moved on to the airlines or something bigger than this."

"Why would I?"

"The pay might be better," I offered. "Don't you want to work on bigger airplanes?"

"I make a good wage now," the mechanic said. "Besides, working on bigger airplanes is the same as repairing small ones except you need a ladder."

"Don't you want to do something more important than changing oil in Cherokees?"

"What could be more important that fixing airplanes for you clowns?"

"I don't know."

"So you're getting itchy feet?" he asked.

"Maybe."

"And you're thinking you should be wearing a fancy uniform and flying a big shiny tube full of admiring passengers?"

"Is there anything wrong with that?"

"Maybe not. It seems to work for other guys who've passed through here."

"That's what I was thinking," I replied.

"If it's a uniform you want," he offered pointing at his oil-stained shop coat, "we've got more of these out back. They've even got names on them."

"Thanks, but it's more than just the clothes."

"Well, let's see what else we can do," he said with a smile. "Instead of Angel saying you have a lesson with Melville in Tango Victor Hotel, we'll rig up a public address system. She can announce that Derry Air Flight Number Two is departing Gate One with First Officer Passmore as your copilot." His grin grew wider. "If it's cabin service you crave, we could have Pilot here ride in the back seat of the Cherokees with a small keg around his neck."

"Thanks, Darcy. I knew I could count on you for an answer."

"Well, you asked," he said with a laugh. Then he leaned forward. "I'll add one more thing. You're a good flying instructor. I've seen some dim-bulb customers see the light after lessons with you. It's not every pilot who can do that. Now you might think it's time to move on but when you're good at something, think about sticking to it." He leaned back. "So there's a reason to stay if you need one but if you're not happy, there's a reason to leave." He drained the last of his coffee and got out of his chair. "I've already said too much. Your student is back and so is my airplane."

I stood up beside him. "I appreciate your comments," I said, "and you're probably right. I should stay."

"Good," he said with a smirk. "I need someone to help me dump the oil on that Cherokee. I'll see you in the shop when you're finished with your student. You can wear a uniform. Do you want to be Huey, Duey or Louey?"

About the Author

Garth Wallace is from St. Catharines, Ontario, near Niagara Falls, where he learned to fly in a Fleet Canuck in 1966. From 1971 until 1990, Garth worked full time at various locations as a flying instructor, bush pilot and corporate pilot. It was during those flying years that he met the colourful characters and lived the humorous experiences that are the basis for his six books of funny flying stories. Garth now lives near Ottawa, Ontario with his wife Liz. He works as a publisher for the Canadian Owners and Pilots Association and flies a Grumman/American Trainer for pleasure.

About the Artist

Francois Bougie's interest in aviation was sparked at an early age by his father who restored several aircraft and constructed two homebuilts. Francois' passion led to a college education as an aircraft maintenance engineer and a career as an electro-mechanical designer in the aerospace industry in Montreal, Quebec. In the 1990s, Francois began applying an artistic talent to aviation art and industrial technical illustrations. His work has been published on several aviation book covers, posters and in aviation magazines. Francois is a licenced pilot. He has owned a Cessna 120 and a Pitts Special. He currently flies a classic 1946 Globe Swift that he restored.

Other books by Garth Wallace

Fly Yellow Side Up

Fly Yellow Side Up is the hilarious story of a suburban flying instructor who moves north seeking the freedom and glory of flying floatplanes. Follow Wallace as he takes a bush pilot job with no floatplane experience and stumbles his way into the fascinating world of wilderness flying.   Soft cover

Pie In The Sky

Laugh with Wallace as he learns that the riches to be found running a small town flying school are in the characters and the memories. In *Pie In The Sky* Wallace discovers cowboy agricultural pilots, Mennonite buggy buzzing and other off-the-wall aviation adventures.   Soft cover

Derry Air

Flying students Marathon Melville and Beautiful Bob, aircraft owner Barnacle Bill, linecrew Huey, Duey and Louey, and the wonderfully sarcastic ground school instructor "Dutch" are some of the crazy characters in *Derry Air,* the hilarious follow-up to *Pie In The Sky*.   Soft cover

The Flying Circus

Get ready to laugh again as Happy Landings presents more funny flying stories by Garth Wallace. *The Flying Circus* is the humourous tale of two instructors who start a flying school with loads of enthusiasm, little business sense and no money.   Soft cover

Don't Call Me a Legend

Don't Call Me a Legend is a true adventure story about a modern-day aviation legend. This heart-warming biography follows Charlie Vaughn as he works his way from sky-gazing farm boy to a world renowned ferry pilot. Fly with Charlie as he delivers a Cessna Skymaster to Botswana, a Twin Otter across the Pacific, a Hawker Siddeley through Russia and many other global adventures.   Hard cover

Blue Collar Pilots

Blue Collar Pilots is a lighthearted joke book that celebrates the real cockpit grunts in aviation - the bush pilots, agricultural pilots, cargo haulers, helicopter pilots, fighter jocks, search and rescue pilots, flying instructors, test pilots, medevac pilots, survey pilots, ferry pilots and water bombers.   Soft cover

All of Garth Wallace's books are published by Happy Landings and are available at pilot supply shops, book stores or directly from the publisher.

Happy Landings
RR # 4, Merrickville
Ontario Canada K0G 1N0
Tel.:613-269-2552 Fax:613-269-3962
Internet: www.happylanding.com
E-mail: books@happylanding.com

Happy Landings accepts telephone or fax orders with VISA or mail orders with cheque or VISA

Other books published by Happy Landings

Papa X-Ray

by Jim Lang

Papa X-Ray is the heartwarming, true story of a trusty old airplane, a family adjusting to life in the far north and a greenhorn pilot learning to fly in the spectacular ruggedness of Canada's Northwest Territories. Follow Jim Lang as he trades a trailer for an airplane and flies it as family transportation through the wilderness around Nahanni Butte.

Soft cover

Ace McCool

by Jack Desmarais

Ace McCool spoofs the airline industry through the laughter-packed exploits of Down East International, a fictional "fly-by-night" operation based in Moncton, New Brunswick. These are the tall tales that brought laughter to thousands of aviators reading *Canadian Aviation* magazine. Now, for the first time, they have been assembled in a collector edition book.

Soft cover

Happy Landings
RR # 4, Merrickville
Ontario Canada K0G 1N0
Tel.:613-269-2552 Fax:613-269-3962
Internet: www.happylanding.com
E-mail: books@happylanding.com